HAIL
MARY

THE 10-STEP PLAYBOOK FOR
REPUBLICAN RECOVERY

By Ford O'Connell

Copyright © 2013 Ford O'Connell
All rights reserved.

ISBN: 1492156884
ISBN 13: 9781492156888

Library of Congress Control Number: 2013915889
CreateSpace Independent Publishing Platform
North Charleston, South Carolina

To my late grandfather Henry Salvatori whose love for America, citizenship and conservative values still inspires me every day.

TABLE OF CONTENTS

INTRODUCTION:

FOURTH … AND LONG

Fourth and long. If this were a football game, that's where the Republicans would be right now. We are on our fourth down in the fourth quarter and trailing by a few touchdowns on the scoreboard. Even now, in the fifth year of an Obama presidency, we're still hanging in there. But the odds are getting longer. And the consequences are potentially severe.

Given the glacial pace of progress in Washington, it no longer seems possible to remake the country in one's ideological image in eight years. But 12 years is another matter. And that's why Republicans should begin now to get their ducks in a row for the 2016 election. Winning in 2016 is not just about which party controls the White House, it is about the future of America and the role that the federal government plays in our everyday lives. If Hillary Clinton or another Democrat wins in 2016 – Obama's liberal America could become permanent. President Obama is already busy trying to refashion the federal judiciary in his image. If the

Democrats hold onto the White House, the America that emerges in 2020 (or 2024) will be unrecognizable.

As we turn our attention to 2016, things aren't looking good for the Grand Old Party at the presidential level. The Republicans have lost the popular vote in five out of the last six presidential elections, and the last time a GOP presidential nominee captured at least 51 percent of the popular vote was 1988 (George H.W. Bush).[1] And with Hillary Clinton, a potential electoral juggernaut waiting in the wings, the Republican Party could find itself locked out of the White House until at least 2024, if not longer.

Many Republicans are under the misguided impression that the GOP is undergoing a cyclical political correction and that the Party finds itself in much the same position it found itself in 1964 when Barry Goldwater was soundly defeated by Lyndon Baines Johnson, but then returned to the White House four years later. Unfortunately, the party is in far worse shape.

While it's true in 2013 that the Republican Party controls 30 of the 50 governors' mansions, a majority of the state legislatures and a majority in the U.S. House of Representatives (thanks to redistricting), the Republican Party is currently a regional party. As University of Virginia professor of politics Larry Sabato points out, Mitt Romney won only six of the nation's 50 largest counties. This drop-off was significant compared to the last two winning Republican presidents, George W. Bush in 2004 — who won 16 of these 50 counties in 2004 — and George H.W. Bush in 1988 — who won a majority of these counties, 29-21, when defeating Michael Dukakis.[2] Republicans are a rural and southern party that is destined to be on the losing end of the ticket given migration trends away from suburbs into cities. There isn't a single Republican member of the House of Representatives who hails from New England anymore.

The various wings of President Obama's permanent campaign — Organizing for Action, the Center for American Progress, etc. — continue to build grassroots support for his policies. And the bully pulpit of the presidency will continue to afford him opportunities to make his case to the American people in a way his rivals cannot. This is momentum in favor of Democrats that Republicans ignore at their own peril.

The Republican Party remains deeply unpopular. As *Washington Post* columnist George Will argues: "It's been well said that you have a political problem when the voters don't like you, but you've got a real problem when the voters think you don't like them."[3] And right now that is where the GOP stands in terms of national politics – a majority of Americans thinks the GOP despises them.

And if the party does not right the ship before 2016, the Republican Party could be demoted to third party status in the very near future – much as the Party currently finds itself in California. And that would be bad for America because a vibrant Republican Party is necessary for a successful two-party political system. The key for the GOP between now and 2016 is to fundamentally rebrand itself as a party of the people, the middle class of Main Street, not just a party of responsible bean counters that is perceived to do Wall Street's bidding.

So what is a well-meaning but underfunded and dis-affected opposition party to do? It needs to refine its ideas — adjust them to new realities where necessary — and find messengers who connect with the people. What else do you do on fourth down when you're desperate for a big play before the clock runs out? We need to go long.

Our side still has the ability to make some clutch plays. The crowd wants to cheer for us. Far more Americans still self-identify as conservatives than as liberals, but the gap has narrowed.[4] America still sees itself as a center-right nation, but it needs leaders and a message to take them where they want to go.

We need to bench some of our players and send some of our coaches packing into the locker room and ultimately back home where they can enjoy eighteen holes of golf every day. We need to rejigger our playbook. Above all, we need to throw some Hail Marys. That's what this book is about – moving votes and winning the White House.

RULE #1:

RONALD REAGAN IS DEAD.
ACCEPT IT.

One of the legendary coaches of the University of Michigan football team was a man named Bo Schembechler. With his folksy style, winning record, and obvious love for his team, Bo was a campus hero – a revered coach not only in Ann Arbor, but also across the nation. His rivalry with Ohio State's Woody Hayes made both men legends. At Michigan, Bo won fame for his strong defensive lines and an offense known for using brute force and a "cloud of dust" to push and scramble its way toward the end zone.

When Bo retired after the Rose Bowl in 1990, many people at the University of Michigan thought he could never be replaced; that Michigan, the winningest program in the history of Division I college football, would never achieve that same glory. But Bo *was* replaced. Michigan went on. The football team scored more victories and more championships, including a co-national championship in 1997 – something Bo never achieved during his 20 years as head coach. Football, like life, went on. The last thing Bo Schembechler would have wanted was for Michigan to live in the past.

I mention this because the Republican Party has not learned this lesson about its own team. We are still waiting for our beloved head coach, Ronald Reagan, to come back out of the locker room and lead us to another victory. No other coach is given a chance to replace him. All who try languish in his shadow. Anyone who tries a different approach is questioned and doubted – "that's not how Ronald Reagan would have done it." This, needless to say, is not the way to build a winning team for the future.

If Republicans want to win big victories again, the first lesson of this book is a painful one and perhaps the most important. Ronald Wilson Reagan is dead. The Gipper died on June 5, 2004, of complications from Alzheimer's Disease coupled with pneumonia at his home in California. He was 93 years old. His wife, Nancy, was at his side. So were his children. His casket laid in state in the U.S. Capitol, with people passing by at a rate of nearly 5,000 per hour.[5] He was eulogized by President George W. Bush and British Prime Minister Margaret Thatcher. The Clintons were there to pay their respects, and so were the Carters. Reagan was then flown to Southern California to the Reagan Presidential Library, where he was laid to rest. These are all facts. There are numerous news outlets that can verify this.

What that means is that the Gipper is not coming back to sweep the GOP up from its doldrums. It's up to us now. The sooner that Republicans can accept that, the better. Unfortunately, that is easier said than done.

A disturbing trend has emerged in the last two Republican presidential primaries. And if it is not dealt with, it could again cripple the Republican Party's White House prospects in 2016. I refer to it as O.R.D. – "Obsessive Reagan Disorder." It is the increasing insistence on demanding that any candidate seeking the White House verify that he is our former president's stylistic and ideological twin.

In the 2008 primary, for example, there wasn't a single candidate running for president who did not mention Reagan's name and genuflect before him as if to seek his blessing. Even the Democrats were talking about Reagan. When Barack Obama said something positive about the Reagan administration – namely that even Ronald Reagan had some good ideas and was "transformational" in a way Bill Clinton, Obama pointedly noted, was not – his main rival, Hillary Clinton, attacked him. And it's doubtful it was out of a sense of loyalty to her husband. If the Democrats can't get over Reagan, it's no wonder that the Republicans are having an even harder time of it.

That same year, John McCain and Mitt Romney fought it out on the airwaves over who was the true heir to Ronald Reagan. A McCain ad ran an old clip of Romney seeming to disparage the Reagan administration. Then an announcer asked, "If we can't trust Mitt Romney on Ronald Reagan, how can we trust him to lead America?"[6]

At a debate at the Reagan Library, McCain used a question about who Ronald Reagan would endorse in the primary to attack Romney again. "Ronald Reagan would not approve of someone who changes their positions depending on what the year is," McCain said.[7]

Four years later, Reagan was the centerpiece again, but this time in a very different story. In a 2012 speech praising his former rival, McCain said Romney and Reagan *shared* the same leadership qualities. "Mitt Romney has the same instincts as Ronald Reagan," said McCain.[8] That year it was Romney's turn to claim the Reagan mantle, and he absurdly attacked his primary rival, Newt Gingrich, as once betraying the Reagan legacy.

All of which begs the question: What does any of this have to do with who should represent the Republican Party in the 21st century?

The Reagan administration has been out of power for decades – and our culture has changed enormously since then. Reagan, for example, did not live in the era of the Internet. I don't think he ever heard of Google or YouTube or Pinterest. He didn't live in the era of tablets and iPhones. He had no position on ObamaCare or stem-cell research or the high costs of prescription drugs. There was no Russia, no country of Georgia or Ukraine or a united Germany. He didn't know about al Qaeda. A whole world has happened, an entire generation has been born, since he was in the saddle and in the White House. The idea that Republicans must be Reagan clones looks pathetically out of touch.

This is the last thing the forward-looking, modest, and practical Reagan would ever want. He didn't wallow in the past. And he believed in the truth.

The truth is that Ronald Reagan is not only dead, he was an imperfect candidate for office. He stumbled in political debates. He lost his place at times. He fell asleep in meetings. He was actually in danger of losing the presidential nomination at one point in 1980 to George H. W. Bush. In 1984 he stumbled in a televised debate against Democrat Walter Mondale which led many to question his stability and age. He was blistered for his management style during the Iran-Contra scandal in 1986. He did not reduce the size of government as president. In fact, it got bigger.

By the way, what Senator McCain implied about Ronald Reagan back in 2008 –that Reagan rarely changed his political positions – is simply not true. This, too, is part of a damaging mythology among Republicans that makes it even more impossible for other candidates to measure up to the sainted Gipper.

The fact is that Ronald Reagan, like any politician, changed his mind about a lot of things. As Governor of California, he signed pro-choice legislation – The Therapeutic Abortion Act – into law, then later said he regretted it. He supported a tax increase in an attempt to balance the state budget, then ran against tax increases. Yet during his administration, there were increased taxes on income, on sales, on alcohol and on cigarettes. As president, Reagan supported the equivalent of amnesty for illegal immigrants. He reached out to the Soviet Union – after pledging a hard line – and signed an arms control agreement that as a candidate he might have rejected. He rejected plans to invade nations such as Panama and Lebanon to protect American national security – a different tact than advanced by other Republicans.

This is how absurd it all has become: If he were starting out as a candidate today, the real Ronald Reagan could not measure up to the Ronald Reagan of myth.

None of this is meant to diminish Reagan's many accomplishments, but to put them into proper, instead of outsized, context. It's dangerous to do it any other way. When we create a false image of Reagan as a perfect person without flaws, there's no way any other Republican can ever hope to match him. Because of course no one is perfect.

I was struck by the toll Obsessive Reagan Disorder had taken on the GOP at the 2013 Conservative Political Action Conference (CPAC) outside of Washington, D.C. just a few months ago. Nearly a decade after his death, Ronald Reagan's name was mentioned a dozen times in the first thirty minutes of the gathering. Rare was a speaker in the three-day conference who did not pay homage to Reagan and the myth of the perfect, unyielding conservative leader.

A giant picture of Reagan adorned the stage whenever anyone spoke. There was, by the way, little or no comparable mention of George W. Bush. No mention of Abraham

Lincoln. No mention of Coolidge, or Hoover, or Teddy Roosevelt or Ford or Nixon or Eisenhower. It was all Reagan.

Enough.

Sometime after the 2014 midterms, a cadre of Republican candidates will officially throw their hats into the ring to be the next president of the United States. Upon doing so they will quickly realize that they have likely bitten off more than they can chew – the endless campaign stops, numerous fund-raisers, and a slew of grueling debates. Of course, the whole ordeal of running to be president looks a lot easier from the sidelines than it is once you are actually on the campaign trail. And if recent history is any indicator – before too long, every candidate who is vying to be the GOP's next standard-bearer will start talking yet again about how Ronald Wilson Reagan influenced their lives and their political ideology. Soon after that, a WWE–style battle royal tends to break out among the candidates as to who best embodies the ideals of Reagan, and is therefore the rightful heir to carry on his legacy.

Frankly the whole exercise is counterproductive, and the Reagan fixation is a drag on the future success of the GOP at the national level. It undermines the candidates because it becomes a crutch for their inability to articulate an actual agenda or a forward-looking vision. And to be perfectly honest, most voters don't really care who is most like Reagan or who Reagan would have endorsed if he were still alive today. They want to know what the candidates are going to do about jobs, kitchen table issues (taxes, energy and education) and national security.

But it doesn't stop with the candidates. GOP primary voters and conservative pundits are also guilty of perpetuating this phenomenon. The GOP must stop chasing the Reagan rainbow, because no candidate is going to measure up to the fabled status that the Republican consciousness has affixed to the 40th President.

In his youth Ronald Reagan played football on his high school team in Dixon, Illinois. He knew as well as anyone that coaches retire, quarterbacks age and the very best linebackers eventually throw in the towel. The best teams don't sit in locker rooms staring at their old trophies and watching old films about past glory. Teams that do that don't win. And he'd be the last person to want that for a Republican Party he helped to shape and build.

Ronald Reagan was a great man. He was a wise man. He was in many ways an ideal leader for his times. But he is gone. Let him rest in peace.

RULE #2:

STOP GIVING A SHIT ABOUT OBAMA'S BIRTHPLACE (AND OBAMA ALTOGETHER)

The New England Patriots are quickly becoming the NFL's equivalent of MLB's New York Yankees. Everyone loves to hate them and their prima donna quarterback, Tom Brady. Among NFL fans southwest of Foxboro, the hatred burns white hot. None of that has slowed the juggernaut. During the 2000s, the Patriots won three Super Bowls and 126 games – the most of any team in one decade in NFL history (including playoffs).[9] Additionally, they have won nine of the last 10 AFC East division titles. People can whine about the infamous "tuck rule" and "Spygate" – but the fact remains that hating the Patriots has not improved a team's ability to beat them on the field over the past decade.

Plenty of other football players have been hated – and continued to pummel opponents. Ben Roethlisberger, Michael Vick, Ndamukong Suh and Tony Romo. But hatred doesn't stop any of their teams from winning games and championships. Hatred doesn't keep their coaches up at night. And hatred doesn't make it easier to beat them. Hate is not a strategy – not in sports, not in life, and definitely not in politics.

One of the great delusions among Republicans in 2012 was that Barack Obama was despised by the American people. Conservatives became so convinced that because his policies were so unabashedly liberal, so mindlessly left-leaning, that a center right nation wouldn't stomach re-electing him. The hatred for Obama was all consuming in certain political circles. An entire electoral strategy, ad campaigns, and outreach efforts were all based on that assessment. And yet it wasn't true.

The last chapter offered Republicans one difficult truth – Ronald Reagan wasn't a saint. This chapter offers another truth that may be even tougher to handle.

Barack Obama isn't the Devil. Not even close. In fact, there are a heck of a lot of politicians worse than he is.

I'm not the only one who thinks so. That was – and is – the general assessment of the American people. We want to believe in our presidents. We want to like them. We want them to succeed. Barack Obama is not an exception.

Through his first term, most public opinion polls consistently showed that a great number of voters, even a majority of them, thought Obama was a smart, appealing person. (Many Americans liked Michelle Obama, too.) They liked the fact that Obama went on ESPN to fill out his March Madness bracket. They laughed at him slow-jamming behind Jimmy Fallon. Instead of having candidates who understood that these were important things to do to connect with voters, our candidates mocked him and derided his efforts to get outside the Beltway bubble as "beneath the dignity of the office."

The reality was that getting media coverage for non-political reasons made Obama, perhaps the most aloof and out of touch president in our history, seem like a normal guy – and a likeable one at that – who had interests outside of the Law of the Sea Treaty and EPA regulations.

Just before the election, when the President had been under attack for months by Republicans, 59 percent of those polled by Pew said Obama connected better with ordinary Americans than Mitt Romney.[10] More people found Obama willing to work with the other party. More voters found Obama honest and truthful. Obama's life story – from the son of a single mother to the first black president of the United States – was a story that made many Americans proud. And still did four years later.

As fellow conservative, and award-winning syndicated columnist Cal Thomas put it with his usual succinctness: "Hating Obama is not … a winning policy."[11] But sometimes, it seemed that was the only strategy that the Republicans had.

Let's be honest – the war on the right to undermine Barack Obama's standing with the American people by questioning everything from the legitimacy of his birth certificate to his religious faith to Donald Trump's zany offer of $5 million for production of his college records to the questionable gaps in his personal history or even his alleged fondness for European-style social democracy (aka socialism) was nothing short of an utter failure. It was a sign of an opposition afraid or unable to run on ideas.

Going after presidents personally like this is almost always a sign of desperation. And almost always a failure.

During the previous administration, the prominent columnist Charles Krauthammer coined the phrase, "Bush Derangement Syndrome." The affliction was defined elsewhere as "the acute onset of paranoia in otherwise normal people in reaction to the policies, the presidency – nay – the very existence of George W. Bush." Symptoms of Bush Derangement Syndrome were said to include such things as:

1. Believing that Bush caused Hurricane Katrina.

2. Believing that Bush was behind 9-11.

3. Calling Bush stupid despite the fact that he has degrees from Harvard and Yale and is a trained fighter pilot."[12]

Over his eight years in the White House George W. Bush was attacked by Democrats as, among other things, a warmonger, a drunk, a coke addict, and a liar. That didn't stop Bush from winning re-election.

Eight years before that, it was Bill Clinton's turn. To Republicans, he was a man accused of (literally) murdering his political enemies, and of running a drug operation in Arkansas.

People loathed Reagan too – an "amiable dunce" was a frequently-cited phrase. They detested Jimmy Carter, the cardigan-wearing Soviet-appeaser. They mocked Gerald Ford, the stumblebum who couldn't navigate a flight of stairs without a catastrophic fall. They savaged Richard Nixon – who went on to win 49 states in 1972 before Watergate brought him down. Some things never change.

In many ways, the ceaseless, increasingly farcical attacks in 2012 on President Obama made Republicans as a whole appear petty. Worse, it caused some voters to become more empathetic towards Obama.

Imagine if, instead of relying on a presumed hatred and animosity toward Obama the person, the Romney campaign ran against Obama the president. Romney and his superPAC allies would not have spent so much time on his personality or his intentions or his background, but focused solely on his competence.

Imagine if Mitt Romney had gone on television and said something like the following: "I think Barack Obama means well. I think he loves his family and loves his country. And

I oppose anyone or any organization that argues to the contrary. Barack Obama's personality is not the problem. His policies are. He may want to do what's right for America, but what his policies have actually done tell a very different story."

That was more fertile territory. While voters found Obama himself likeable, they found his job performance lacking. Obama's job approval rating was just under 50 percent on average, according to Gallup, about as low as Gerald Ford and Jimmy Carter (both of whom lost their bids for another term). [13]

There is a lesson here for Republicans in 2016 – when they may face another polarizing, divisive candidate again. Don't go after political enemies personally, but on ideas and philosophy. Concede their good intentions. Kill them, in effect, with kindness. In doing so, Republicans would be following the tradition of other effective political leaders in dealing with their opponents – out of sympathy or pity, not animus or bile.

Franklin Delano Roosevelt was constantly under attack by Republicans – for being an aristocrat, a socialist, a liar, and on and on. FDR usually tossed the attacks aside with a shrug. But when Republicans circulated a story that FDR had sent a military ship to retrieve his dog, Fala, at considerable taxpayer expense, FDR pounced on the false story to make his opponents look foolish.

"These Republican leaders have not been content with attacks on me, or my wife, or on my sons," he said in a speech.

"No, not content with that, they now include my little dog, Fala. Well, of course, I don't resent attacks, and my family don't [sic] resent attacks, but Fala does resent them ... I am accustomed to hearing malicious falsehoods about myself ... But I think I have a right to resent, to object, to libelous statements about my dog!"[14]

Similarly when Democrats attacked Ronald Reagan for stumbling in a debate and suggested he was going senile, Reagan turned the attack back on his opponents with a good-natured quip. "I want you to know that also I will not make age an issue of this campaign," he said at his next debate, with Democrat Walter Mondale in 1984. "I am not going to exploit, for political purposes, my opponent's youth and inexperience."[15]

So much more can be accomplished in politics with good humor and a little self-awareness. In that regard, it's time that Republicans faced a few uncomfortable facts about the man they have tried and failed to defeat. Twice.

Fact #1: President Obama was elected twice with a majority of the popular vote and more than 300 electoral votes.

Fact #2: The majority of the American people like Obama and want him to do well.

Fact #3: The American people like Obama more than they like any Republican we can mention.

Fact #4: President Obama is a Christian.

Fact #5: President Obama was born in the United States of America.

And of course the most important fact is this one: Barack Obama will never be on a presidential ballot again. Let him go. Again, all together now, *let him go.*

That's right. I meant that. Here's an idea for Republicans at least for the next year or so: Forget about Barack Obama. Don't mention his name. Get rid of the crutch you use to raise money and appeal to your own base and instead do the hard work of developing a philosophy and a 21st century alternative to the Democratic Party. Disregard the easy story and Drudge link traffic about the ring on Obama's finger that has verses from the Qur'an on it. Snopes.com must have gigabytes of articles about the ridiculousness our side has tried to throw at Obama in the vain hope that something, somehow might stick.

For once, let Obama sink or swim on his own.

One would think by now most on the right would have gotten the message. But at CPAC 2013 you could have fooled me. This was best evidenced by Sarah Palin comparing Obama to Bernie Madoff, coupled with her suggestion that background checks for guns are a "dandy idea" so long as we "started with [Obama's]."[16] Enough is enough. This has to stop. It hurts the GOP brand and does nothing to further the Republican cause.

Unfortunately, ceasing this childish behavior does not mean President Obama is not bent on pulverizing Congressional Republicans and controlling both legislative chambers following the 2014 midterm elections in an effort to cement his progressive legacy (end climate change, turn back the rising oceans, give more power to unions, etc). Because he is. Even *The Washington Post*, an ardent Obama supporter, admits this much.[17] It's why the president's brain trust set up "Organizing For Action," a ruthlessly political organization that will send mobs of eager college freshman to your door to sign petitions and collect email addresses – even though the White House emphatically denies it.

And total annihilation at the polls is not an impossible scenario. Let's remember Congress' approval is abysmal (high teens) and the Republican Party brand is not much better – hovering around the 30s, according to a recent WSJ/NBC poll.[18]

So the only way for the Republicans to stave off Obama's designs on controlling the House of Representatives, thereby pushing more economically destructive policies, is to intellectually defeat Obama's policies (as has occurred thus far with the sequester) or to find common ground with the White House. Of course, the Republicans can hope that Obama could fall flat on his face, but I frankly don't like those odds given that he is a skilled campaigner.

And trust me, the White House will resort to every trick in the book to portray Republicans as the party of "No" by continuing to lob legislation at them that seeks to make them look out of step with the American people.

Eventually, Republicans will be forced to dramatically shift gears. They will have to become a party that is for things, not just against excessive government spending and ballooning deficits. Right now their best bet is to concentrate on a 21st century middle class agenda rooted in jobs, immigration reform, modernizing entitlements, energy security and education.

ROE V. WADE IS HERE TO STAY

Most coaches, when they have a winning strategy, run it over and over until an opposing team can stop it. Vince Lombardi's "Packers Sweep," for example, perhaps the most well-known play in football, helped the Green Bay Packers dominate their opponents for a decade, leading to five league championships and two victories in the Super Bowl. In truth, there's nothing spectacular about the play but it worked, time and time again.

The analogy applies to politics too. Democrats have a winning play. They've used it to increasing success in the last few elections, and they are going to keep using it as long as their opposition can't figure out a way to stop it. They are running up their margins with women voters, specifically unmarried women, by talking about abortion. More to the point, they scare female voters about plots, real and imagined, by Republican men to take abortion rights away.

The Democrats use the abortion issue every year against Republicans and, except in "Deep Red" areas where anti-abortion sentiment is strongest, it has helped them enormously. Pollsters from the Gallup organization analyzed the "gender gap" in 2012. The survey, conducted in swing states, showed that women were most concerned about "gender specific issues," "abortion," "government policies concerning birth control," and "equal pay" over major 2012 election issues like "jobs" and "the economy."

Consider what an amazing accomplishment that was. In an election in which America's economy was struggling, Americans were out of work by the millions, and housing prices continued to sag, the Obama campaign convinced nearly half the electorate to concentrate on something else. "Abortion" is the shiny object the President used to distract voters. Here's what else the Gallup poll found:

- "There are a number of possible reasons for the increase in the gender gap this year. For example, Romney's business background may have been more appealing to men than to women. Obama's campaign stressed maintaining the social safety net, raising taxes on the wealthy, maintaining abortion rights, and requiring healthcare coverage for contraception – all in contrast to Romney's more conservative positions on these issues of potential interest to women."

- "The Democratic Party will likely attempt to secure Obama's election advantage among women by carrying forward the themes that seemed to work in future elections at all levels of government. It remains to be seen whether and how the Republican Party will change course to try to broaden its appeal to women without forfeiting the strong support of men."[19]

The effect of Obama's abortion campaign was particularly strong among single women who, according to some estimates, now comprise roughly 23 percent of the overall electorate.[20] These voters increasingly have moved to the Democrats. In 2004, John Kerry won 62 percent of their vote. In 2008, President Obama carried 70 percent of unmarried women. In 2012 he dipped only slightly, capturing 67 percent of the single women vote.[21] The reason that the Democrats saturate the airwaves on issues like abortion and contraception is because single women, as a voting bloc, tend to pay less attention to political news. According to surveys, more than 72 percent say they have "moderate to no interest in politics."[22] It is therefore easier to attract their votes with alarmist, single-issue campaign ads, since they are less familiar with the positions and policy arguments of various candidates.

But just as importantly for Republicans, the "abortion" issue has become a needless distraction from their real agenda. If Mitt Romney were being honest, "restricting abortion" would probably be the absolute last item on his agenda – if it were on the list at all. For months, Romney tied himself in knots over the issue – having to explain away the pro-choice views he held while running for office in Massachusetts, then explaining his conversion to a pro-life position, then having to discuss, explain, or apologize for any statement he made since that deviated even slightly. At one point during the Republican primaries he endorsed a stricter anti-abortion position than he ever had before, and then tried to walk it back after he won the GOP nomination. He was battered endlessly in the media for his supposed waffling which contributed to a damaging image of Romney the political chameleon.

Unless Republicans want to keep losing single women by nearly 40 points, they need to change the way they react to the Democratic playbook. And they need to come up with some innovative plays of their own.

The first item on that agenda: facing the facts. Like it or not, on abortion the country has come to a consensus. On the 40th Anniversary of the landmark Supreme Court decision, *Roe v. Wade,* a Pew poll found that 63 percent of registered voters said they would not like to see a woman's right to an abortion completely overturned. The number has been unchanged for decades. In 2003, that percentage was 62 percent. In 1992, twenty years ago, 60 percent of registered voters polled said the same thing. In the Pew poll, at least, that number included 48 percent of Republicans who said they did not want *Roe* overturned and 55 percent of voters identified themselves as Catholics.[23]

Only a handful of politicians in either party would dare to directly attack something that had received close to super-majority support in the nation. That means that the right to abortion will continue to exist. It may come with stricter limits in some states than in others. But the country does not want abortion completely outlawed. A majority in Congress lacks the political will to do it and likely could not get any new law past a president of either party, even if they summoned the courage. The United States Supreme Court, even under a conservative majority, has declined to overturn *Roe v. Wade* repeatedly. Like it or not, it is the law of the land. And that's that.

Yet the Republican Party has somehow seemed to move even further in the opposite direction than ever before. The party continues to endorse official language in its platform such as the following: "The unborn child has a fundamental individual right to life which cannot be infringed. We support a human life amendment to the Constitution and endorse legislation to make clear that the 14th Amendment's protections apply to unborn children."

To a lot of conservatives, of course, there's nothing wrong with that language. But if you believe abortion might be permissible in cases of rape or incest or the endangerment of the mother's life, that's not official Republican Party policy. As *The New York Times*, no friend to Republicans, put it, "Republicans approved platform language on Tuesday calling for a constitutional amendment outlawing abortion with no explicit exceptions for cases of rape or incest."[24]

The number of people in America who agree with such an absolutist position on abortion is 20 percent, according to a Gallup survey. Since Gallup has asked the question – "do you believe abortion should be outlawed in all circumstances?" – that number has been roughly constant. In 1977, the number was also 20 percent.[25]

Needless to say, a party that promotes so heavily a position that is opposed by 80 percent of the country is not on the winning side of the debate.

The perception of Republican extremism on abortion allows the mainstream media to play up the issue on behalf of the Democrats. Every politically astute person in the nation was aware of Republican Senate candidate Todd Akin's comment about so-called "legitimate rape." Answering a question about whether abortion should be legal in cases of rape, he infamously replied, "If it's a legitimate rape, the female body has ways to try to shut that whole thing down."[26] That remark alone – defended by many conservatives – may have cost him the race against Democrat Claire McCaskill. Then in Indiana, Republican Senate candidate Richard Mourdock made an equally infamous statement: "I think even when life begins in that horrible situation of rape, that it is something that God intended to happen."[27] He too was defended by some conservatives. Those are the kind of dumb comments that played into the Democrats' hands. This was made possible because Republicans have created an image of themselves on abortion as uncompromising extremists. That's deadly for many female voters who might otherwise support the GOP on pocketbook issues alone. And given the current perception that the GOP brand is "inflexible" and the general overall perspective that Republicans "don't care about people," this should be a major area of concern.

I am not advocating that the next Republican presidential nominee should be pro-choice, because the social conservative wing of the base will walk away (and a party without a base is not a party). But I am saying that touting how pro-life you are (particularly in the primary in a YouTube era) could be like flying an airplane into an active volcano. And Republicans can count on Democrats to lay the bait and set the trap. The GOP would be wise not to get involved in debates about constitutional amendments banning abortion (as occurred during the 2012 GOP presidential primary), and should strip it from the Party's platform altogether. To avoid losing support of social conservatives, Republicans should support more innocuous, and less sweeping pro-life language instead.

Case in point was the recent reauthorization of the "Violence Against Women" measure (which was less than ideal legislation). The House Republican leadership had the good sense to allow the bill to pass because they recognized the power of naming legislation. Combined with how little the average voter knows, taking a stand on the Violence Against Women Act would have easily allowed the Democrats to drag the Republican brand and the Party's eventual 2016 standard-bearer further down into the mud.

Between now and Election Day 2016, one can expect more of this legislative chicanery and other trumped-up "gotcha" moments on the part of Democrats. These wedge issues will be used to take down Republicans in vulnerable districts and to ensure a third straight term for a Democratic president. If the GOP doesn't recognize that the Democrats' Packers Sweep play revolves around "women's rights," they'll soon find themselves out of the game altogether.

RULE #4:

HUG THE GAYS (NO, REALLY)

The last thing on earth the Republican Party would brand itself as is "the party of gays." And yet if it weren't for gay and lesbian Republicans, George W. Bush likely would not have been re-elected President of the United States. And if it weren't for the votes his party received from gays, John Boehner probably would not be Speaker of the House today.

In 2004, when Bush narrowly defeated Democrat John Kerry, Bush did so with the support of 23 percent of gay voters, according to exit polls.[28] Moreover, at least one of Bush's top campaign strategists, Ken Mehlman, was a homosexual – one of a large number of (mostly) closeted Republicans working in Washington, D.C.

In 2010, when Republicans retook control of the United States Congress, and John Boehner reclaimed the Speaker's gavel for the GOP, they did so with the support of 31 percent of gay voters.[29]

No one knows exactly how many people in America are gay or lesbian – but it's a number in the millions, and by some estimates, as many as nine million.[30] With that many self-identified voters (a population roughly the size of New Jersey), the gay vote is not likely to singlehandedly swing a presidential election, but it certainly could affect a tight election, particularly in some key swing states like Florida and Ohio.

The vast majority of gays, of course, are Democrats, and they have formed a powerful and influential voting bloc. But there is no reason in the world that more from the gay community should not be part of a Republican coalition. In some ways, they are a natural constituency for the GOP. They tend to have higher incomes and are more fiscally conservative, have higher education levels, and have a libertarian streak. They also organize, contribute financially to political campaigns, and they tend to vote.

The Democrats understand this far better than Republicans. In fact, Democratic leaders are determined to turn the "gay vote" into as solid a bloc for them as the "black vote" or, increasingly, the "Hispanic vote." And if they are successful, the consequences for the GOP would be deadly. Without the support of gays, closeted or otherwise, Republicans simply cannot win many elections. So why then are the Republicans so determined to help the Democrats accomplish their goal? Why are they working so hard to diminish and sabotage their own potential supporters?

With significant prompting from the Democrats and their allies in the media, America's attitude toward gay rights in general is changing dramatically. The Democrats are pushing for broader and more aggressive recognition of the gay lifestyle, while Republican leaders, cautious and conservative, appear increasingly out of step. At the core of this shift is generational change.

Consider that when NBA player Jason Collins came out as gay, he received immediate support from Bill Clinton and Barack and Michelle Obama. Prominent Republicans were notably silent. Most GOP pundits sneered at the announcement and the media's portrayal of "bravery." But, like it or not, it was a major moment in American culture, as the first male athlete playing a major professional sport stepped out and announced that he was gay. Furthermore, it wasn't even that controversial, at least according to Americans. An ABC News/Washington Post poll found seven in 10 Americans supporting his decision to publicly disclose his sexuality. The ABC poll also found a majority supporting the Boy Scouts of America's plan to admit gay scouts – a measure most Republicans actively and loudly oppose.[31]

The gay marriage question is showing the GOP in even greater trouble. A Pew Research Center survey just before the Supreme Court struck down the Defense of Marriage Act (DOMA) found that "nearly three-quarters of Americans – 72% – say that legal recognition of same-sex marriage is 'inevitable.'" Those results included 59 percent of gay marriage opponents. The same survey found that support for legalizing gay marriage continues to grow, as over half (51 percent) of Americans favor allowing gays and lesbians to marry legally for the first time in Pew polling. Eighty-seven percent of respondents said they personally knew someone who was gay or lesbian – up from 61 percent in 1993.[32] If voters perceive Republicans to be hostile to their friends or acquaintances who are gay, it could easily shape their entire outlook on the party. There is even more cause for concern when looking at the numbers among the GOP rank-and-file. Among self-identified Republicans (and Republican-leaning independents) aged 18-49 in a recent Washington Post/ABC News poll, a majority — yes, a majority — said same sex marriage should be legal.[33] Polling also suggests that this is not just a fad – every generation is growing more accepting of the idea.

Those findings were echoed by an NBC News/Wall Street Journal survey conducted in April 2013. That poll found 53 percent in favor of same sex marriage and an even larger majority, 63 percent, expressing the belief that the federal government should recognize gay marriages as legal in various states, such as California.[34]

Former Vice President Dick Cheney came out in support of gay marriage, as did former First Lady Laura Bush. Ohio Senator Rob Portman also shifted his position after his own son revealed he was gay.

But tolerance for gay rights does not seem to be the message most Americans are hearing from the GOP these days.

At this year's Conservative Political Action Conference, CPAC, the gay Republican group GOProud was excluded from being an event co-sponsor, leading some well-known Republicans to skip the conference over concerns about intolerance and an ever-narrowing definition of what constitutes "conservative."

This was followed by the May 2013 resignation of Pat Brady, the Illinois Republican Party chairman, after he "was savagely attacked by his fellow Republicans" – as the media put it anyway – for his personal support of gay marriage. "I think there are people in the party who don't necessarily agree with me," Brady said before he was forced to step down, "but the point is ... we're a party that welcomes all ideas. You don't have to be exactly a platform Republican to be welcome in the party, and that's the direction we're taking the party."[35]

In response to such comments, some top Republicans in the state issued several calls for his resignation, and orchestrated efforts to oust him as party chairman, along with protests and personal attacks. The whole affair cemented an image in Americans' minds of a party out of step with the country, intolerant and, worse, hateful. A 2013 WSJ/NBC poll found only 22 percent of the voters agreed with the Republican Party's positions on social and cultural issues – 15 points lower than the Democrats.[36]

The growing view of a "gay-hating" GOP is taking its toll. The number of gays voting Republican, which had been rising for years, is now beginning to drop. In the 2012 election, exit polls showed that only 22 percent of gays supported Mitt Romney, a 9-point decline in the Republican vote since 2010. Overall, Obama held a more than three-to-one advantage in exit polls among voters who identified themselves as gay, lesbian or bisexual.[37] It doesn't take a genius to see that these numbers are trending in the wrong direction.

The problem is only going to worsen. Social conservatives and older Republicans can fight it all they want, but same-sex marriage laws are going to spread. The practice is already legal in 13 states and the District of Columbia, and the Supreme Court DOMA decision will likely pave the way for others to follow. The acclaimed political analyst Nate Silver says his opinion data project foresees 32 states legalizing gay marriage by 2016 and 44 states by 2020.[38] Simply put, the GOP is leaving votes on the table, because as conservative pundit Jonah Goldberg notes: "Telling people they are free to be unhappy isn't all that persuasive."[39]

A sudden flip on gay questions isn't going to lead to a sea of change at the polls among gay voters. Even if the GOP endorsed same-sex marriage, it would be difficult for Republicans to capture a sizeable majority of the gay vote. As New York University professor Patrick Egan notes: "Many [gay voters] aren't swingable because they have liberal positions. They have liberal positions on a whole bunch of issues besides gay rights."[40] But even if Republicans can't win a majority of gay votes – at least in the next few decades, they can start broadening their base of support, especially among young people.

The GOP's "traditional marriage" stance hurts it the most with voters under 40 (particularly those between 18 and 29). Staunch opposition to gay rights runs counter to libertarian principals, which is what attracted many of the Republican Party's young people to it in the first place. Individuals should be able to choose with whom they want to associate, and with whom they can start families, without an overbearing federal government standing in their way. At the state level it's a no-brainer. The Republican Party is either the party of the Tenth Amendment and federalism, or it's not. If states want to have referendums and pass legislation allowing their citizens to express their opinion on gay issues, they should have every right to do so under our Constitution.

Aside from a libertarian argument, there is, of course, a conservative case for gay marriage, which some brave GOP pundits are beginning to make. The notion that married folks tend to vote Republican seems to hold true regardless of how the family unit is constructed.

A Gallup survey found that nearly half of LGBT Romney supporters (49 percent) are married or living with a partner, compared with 39 percent of Obama LGBT supporters. The utility aspects of a family unit cause people to reorder their priorities and vote GOP; among the big selling points: "financial success without government interference."[41]

Whether you're gay or straight: Marriage promotes outcomes that conservatives should support – stable homes with committed couples who take care of themselves without government intrusion. We know the benefits to society of stable marriages, and we celebrate them. Our fellow Republicans should be strengthening this institution, not stifling it with roadblocks.

If the most fundamental building block of any society is the nuclear family, Republicans should be doing what they can to strengthen it, to encourage more people to commit to each other in a way that increases long-term economic stability and allows children to grow up with two parents – even if both are of the same sex.

By all accounts, young people should have flocked to the Republican ticket in the 2012 election, as they did in 1980 toward Ronald Reagan and away from a recession-plagued Carter administration. Facing record unemployment close to 20 percent for their age cohort, they should have been lining in up droves to toss out an administration that made no headway in reducing youth employment and evinced even less interest in doing so.[42] And yet it shouldn't be too much of a mystery as to why the GOP didn't win them over. Among Republicans there is no sense of the social reality that young people experience in their high schools and colleges and careers – and that is one in which gays are overwhelmingly welcomed.

I am keenly aware that the 2016 GOP presidential nominee will likely not back same-sex marriage, because older, more conservative primary-goers will exact a toll for a position out of step with their values. So the best path forward until gay marriage becomes more commonplace in the GOP – and that day will be coming given the inevitable demographic trends – is to show tolerance towards gays and lesbians.

That doesn't mean Mitt Romney traipsing through Dupont Circle at the front of a gay pride parade. It means first and foremost changes in tone when talking about gay issues. "If you're involved in the gay and lesbian lifestyle, it's bondage. Personal bondage, personal despair and personal enslavement," Michelle Bachmann once said.[43] First of all, eliminate "bondage" from the lexicon altogether. Even when disagreeing with those who support gay marriage, talk about "respect." And don't drum out the minority voices (currently, but not for long) in the party who support gay rights.

RULE #5:

KILL IMMIGRATION REFORM, KILL THE GOP.

In a nation as diverse as the United States of America, being able to relate to different audiences is critical. Sports leagues, which thrive off of fan support, understand this. The NFL has launched a number of initiatives around Hispanic Heritage Month to expand its fan base and keep the sport healthy. Some of these initiatives include launching NFL Español, creating participatory programs geared specifically towards Hispanic youth, broadcasting live Spanish coverage of games on Univision Radio, and securing deals with Spanish TV networks like ESPN Deportes. The NBA has done the same, seeing Latino-Americans as the key to keeping a strong fan base and raising interest in professional basketball. They're led by the Lakers and the Heat, who, knowing their audience, have seen huge revivals in their fan bases.

In politics though, ethnic "outreach" comes most frequently in the form of gaffes. Sometimes they're entirely innocent. (Think of George McGovern asking for "a kosher hot dog and a glass of milk.") Sometimes they're a little less innocent. (Think of Joe Biden discussing Indian immigrants and saying "you cannot go to a 7-Eleven or a Dunkin' Donuts unless you have a slight Indian accent.")[44] And sometimes they cost you the Texas Republican presidential primary.

Gerald Ford learned that last lesson the hard way in 1976. At a photo op in San Antonio at the Alamo, he ate a tamale. Harmless, right? Well, not if you fail to remove the tamale's inedible husk. Ford sent an accidental signal to the Hispanic community that he was so unfamiliar with their culture; he didn't even know how to eat a tamale. "There were two things I learned in Texas," said President Ford, shortly after losing the state's primary to Ronald Reagan. "One is – never underestimate your opponent, and two is – always shuck the tamale."[45]

Unfortunately for the GOP, most of our candidates are equally clueless when it comes to reaching out to Hispanic voters. Most Republicans don't speak to their concerns (in English or Spanish). They don't visit their churches and community centers. They don't ask for their vote. And they don't get it.

Oh – and they don't support immigration reform.

Now some of you may think immigration reform means flouting American laws, sacrificing American jobs, and driving down American wages. I'm not here to tell you whether you're right or wrong. I'm here to tell you: Get over it.

If Republicans block immigration reform, they will alienate a generation or more of the fastest growing ethnic group in the United States. They've already failed to win a majority in five of the last six presidential elections. If they permanently alienate Hispanics, they may never win another one.

See if you can figure out the answer to this riddle. Hispanics are the largest minority group in America, but they won't be the largest minority 30 years from now. Why? Because white Americans will be.

If you got that one right, let's see if you can go two for two. What grew by 2.5 percent in 2011? I'll give you a hint: It wasn't Obama's anemic economy. The answer is – the population of Hispanics in the United States.[46] In a single year. With few signs of slowing down. Hispanics are currently 16.7 percent of the nation, and by 2060, nearly one in three U.S. residents will be Hispanic.[47] By that point in time, non-Hispanic whites will be a minority, as they already are among American newborns.[48]

Last question. What does this mean for the GOP? It's the question that matters most, and its answer depends on which road the Republicans choose.

One choice is the road to irrelevancy, and we can choose this road by simply following the Mitt Romney playbook. Reject the DREAM Act and immigration reform. Talk about "self-deportation." Denigrate the "47 percent." Spend far less on Spanish-languages ads than your opponent. And win just 27 percent of the Hispanic vote.[49]

I call it the road to irrelevancy not because Republicans are currently unable to win a presidential election with just 27 percent of Hispanics. With a better candidate, any number of winning coalitions without Hispanics was imaginable in 2012. The problem is that, in the future, Republicans will not be able to come *close* to winning a presidential election with just 27 percent of the Hispanic vote, regardless of the coalition they put together.

Battleground states like Florida, Colorado, Nevada, and New Mexico have large Hispanic populations. George W. Bush won each of them. But unless a Republican candidate can significantly increase the party's appeal to Hispanics, these states won't even be competitive. Growth in the Hispanic populations of these states far outstrips the white voter base of the GOP.

In their wake will be a new pair of battleground states: Arizona and (gulp) Texas. They both border Mexico. They both have millions of Hispanics. And they both would have cast their electoral votes for Barack Obama if Hispanics had doubled their share of the American electorate – as they will in the future.[50]

Unfortunately, these trends may be less than obvious to Republican congressmen, because many of their congressional districts are among the only places the percentage of Hispanics is not growing. When you gerrymander a district to protect Republicans, you exclude Democratic voters. And when you exclude Democratic voters, you often end up excluding minorities. What's left is a district that's more conservative and whiter. You get Rep. Daniel Webster's Florida district, which went from 57 percent white to 66 percent. (Undoubtedly the original Daniel Webster's Massachusetts district was even whiter.) Congressman Pete Session's Texas district jumped even higher – up 11 percent from 42 percent white to 53 percent. And not to be outdone, Rep. Pat Tiberi's Ohio district rocketed from 68 percent white to 88 percent. This is how the white share of the average Republican House district nationwide increased 2 percent between 2004 and 2012, while the white share of the nationwide electorate fell by 5 percent.[51]

The good news is that even though only 48 percent of voters cast ballots for Republican House candidates in 2012, 54 percent of those candidates won.[52] The bad news is that you can't gerrymander a presidential election. About the same percentage of voters cast ballots for Mitt Romney that year, but he lost in a landslide.

Fortunately, we need not follow the Mitt Romney model down the road to irrelevancy. Instead, Romney can be our Jacob Marley – a man doomed by the bad choices we still have time to avoid. Romney's candidacy wore "the chains he forged in life" – or at least the ones he forged in Iowa. But for us, there is still time to learn the lesson Romney learned too late. Embrace the DREAM Act and immigration reform. Reject "self-deportation." Show up in Hispanic communities and on Spanish-language airwaves. Speak to their concerns. Pray with them and dine with them (and remember to shuck your tamale). Find common ground. Earn their votes. And win elections.

This road to victory begins with an embrace of immigration reform. There's no question our immigration system is broken. Today, it is easier to come here illegally than legally. Border security is a mess. Extremely high-paying technology jobs go unfilled for lack of qualified applicants. Low-skilled jobs are similarly hard to fill in some areas.

Immigrants – even illegal immigrants – come to America for many of the same freedoms and opportunities our ancestors sought. We must find a way to let in the workers we need and welcome the workers we have. And while we're at it, it's worth remembering – and reminding our party members – that whether your family's first immigrants were brought to America on a pilgrim's boat or a coyote's truck, we are all God's children.

An embrace of immigration reform would open the door to a GOP that can survive and thrive. Remember that George W. Bush supported reform and won 44 percent of Hispanic votes in 2004. Over 40 percent of Obama's Hispanic voters have sometimes voted Republican in the past, and even more of them tell pollsters they will consider doing so again if the Republican Party takes the lead in passing immigration reform.[53]

Embracing immigration reform makes even more sense when you consider the impossibility of the alternatives. We're not going to deport 12 million people. We're not going to seal our nearly 2,000-mile southern border. We're not going to stop being the Promised Land for immigrants. Some version of immigration reform is going to happen. The only question is whether Republicans are going to get any of the credit for it.

Let's also be clear about the limits of embracing reform. It is the beginning of the road to victory, not the end. It is necessary, but not sufficient. Republicans will have to convince Hispanics that our platform and plans hold as much promise for them as for whites. That GOP economic principles will create more jobs than the Democrats' would. That our education principles will produce better schools than the Democrats' would. That Republican national security principles will protect all of us more effectively than the Democrats' would.

We already have the right principles, and with the right messengers, we can explain those principles and win these arguments with any audience willing to listen. The problem is that, as Senator Marco Rubio points out, you can't convince people to listen on economic policy if they "think you want to deport their grandmother."[54]

If Republicans get immigration reform right, there is every reason to believe that large numbers of Hispanic voters will be open to our message of low taxes, less regulation, balanced budgets, family values, and a strong defense. This is a community in which the family and family values are strong. Sixty-three percent of Hispanic family households are married couples, and 67 percent of Hispanic children live with two parents.[55] It's also a community of entrepreneurs. When you think about it, there isn't much that's more entrepreneurial than risking everything to build a better life in a new country. It is that entrepreneurial spirit that caused the number of Hispanic-owned businesses to rise 43 percent in just a five-year period from 2002 to 2007.[56] As the Hispanic business community rapidly grows, so should the number of Hispanic Republicans – just as soon as they know we don't want to deport their grandmothers!

I'm convinced that conservative principles are winning principles. But to win with them, Republicans will have to follow the advice of Governor Haley Barbour and "get serious about aggressively campaigning for the Hispanic vote."[57] That means more townhalls in Hispanic neighborhoods, more advertising in Spanish, and more courting of Hispanic community leaders.

If Mitt Romney lit the light on the road to irrelevance, a New Mexican Republican named Steve Pearce is carrying the light for us to follow on the road to victory. He has won election five times – each time with at least 55 percent of the vote and more than 40 percent of Hispanics – in a district that is nearly half Hispanic and only a third Republican.[58] And he's done so without supporting many of the elements of immigration reform. Pearce told Fox News Latino he goes "out into the community." As Pearce described it, "Talk with them about family, about the economy, you build up a sense of knowledge about who you are, I explain my views of the economy, of the world, in pretty down to earth terms." The

Pearce model means we "go to where it's not comfortable, where people will ask you the hard questions."[59]

Of course, when we answer those questions, we need answers that don't alienate the audience. That does not mean abandoning conservative principles. It simply means losing the hardness and elitism that has too often infected the tone with which those principles have been advocated.

Romney never seemed to get this. There was the "47 percent" gaffe, "self-deportation," his liking to fire people and Ann's two Cadillacs. It all added up to a candidate who couldn't connect. In the end, it's no mystery why President Obama was able to pummel him 81 percent to 18 percent among voters who wanted their president to "care about people like me."[60] (The real mystery is which voters *don't* want their president to care about them!)

Among those 81 percent are immigrants like Irma Guereque. At 60 years old, she's seen her ups and downs since leaving Mexico to start a new life in Las Vegas. She bought a home but lost it when the recession caused a casino to cut her work hours. Irma said, a lot of politicians are "only thinking of the rich, and not the poor, and that's not right. We need opportunities for everyone."[61]

Republican principles are the recipe for those opportunities. But if we kill immigration reform, we'll never get a chance to prove it.

As the NFL and NBA know, keeping a healthy fan base requires knowing your audience.

And shucking your tamale.

LEAVE THE SIDESHOWS TO DONALD TRUMP

In New Hampshire, on January 7, 2012, at the 14th of 20 Republican presidential debates, George Stephanopoulos asked: "Governor Romney, do you believe that states have the right to ban contraception?"

To fair-minded viewers at home, tuning in to hear answers to the questions on their minds, the question was typical of the moderator's "excessive and biased line of questioning." But from the perspective of someone trying to derail the Romney campaign, Stephanopoulos's question was a clever trap. If Romney had said states have the right to ban birth control, it would sound like he *wants* to ban birth control. If Romney had said states don't have the right, he would be endorsing the constitutional "right to privacy," which protects abortion. For Romney, it was a guaranteed lose-lose.

Romney tried to point out the obvious – that no state or candidate wants to ban contraceptives – but Stephanopoulos badgered Romney for three and a half minutes. He was proud of the trap he had set, and he was only interested in making sure the Republican frontrunner fell into it.

Ten months later, again in New Hampshire – where once upon a time a Republican (George W. Bush) actually beat a Democrat (Al Gore) – female voters chose Barack Obama over Mitt Romney by a 16-point margin.[62]

The 16-point margin and the debate question about contraception are connected. The question reinforced in the minds of some voters – particularly the minds of some female voters – the lie that Romney was waging a "war on women." Obama's surrogates and supporters told women that Republicans like Romney would take away their birth control, were insensitive to rape victims, and opposed equal pay for equal work. Once the candidate of "hope," Obama won by appealing to women's worst fears. And he did it with a big assist from George Stephanopoulos.

Here are just a few questions to consider. Why was George Stephanopoulos – a former hack for Michael Dukakis, Dick Gephardt, and Bill Clinton – allowed to moderate the 14th Republican presidential debate? And why were there 14 Republican presidential debates before the first ballot was cast in New Hampshire?

The answers – he shouldn't be, and there shouldn't be – strike me as obvious. But unless we fix this ludicrous process, unless we change the debates from a self-destructive reality show to a sensible forum for the discussion of important issues, history will repeat itself. Republicans' nominee in 2016 will be damaged goods before the general election season even begins.

As the 2012 election demonstrated, it matters who exactly is carrying the standard of the party. To win, the party needs more than good ideas. But the 2012 primary demonstrated another important factor, one that Republicans would do well to remember before they even get into general election mode and find themselves campaigning for a party that's already been set back. A successful primary season in 2016 will mean much more than the final candidate: It will mean leaving the sideshows behind; the ones that distract from the real issues that concern an American public with a short attention span and in the end, bog down the GOP candidate before he or she even gets on the campaign trail.

The "marketplace of ideas" is important, but not if some of the losing "ideas" are still associated with the winning candidate. When the primary season becomes a fight-to-the-death WWE SmackDown event, the GOP's standard-bearer won't walk out of the arena unscathed. (Don't be fooled by Mitt's unruffled blue blazer, white dress shirt, and slick hair.) If they don't pay attention to Rule #6, they'll probably be banged up and shell-shocked before they even get into the game.

John Gagliardi understood this rule of "limited contact before the actual game." Who's John Gagliardi? Only the winningest college football coach in history. Inducted into the College Football Hall of Fame in 2006, Gagliardi racked up 30 conference championships, four national titles, and a record 489 wins in primarily Division III football by asking a simple, but controversial coaching question: "If we tackle in practice, who do we hurt? Our own quarterback and running back."[63]

If it didn't work, then there's no way such a strange football concept would have survived. But it did work. 489 times. As a former player himself, Gagliardi wondered why teams should run themselves ragged in practice, playing at full speed with endless hard-hitting tackle drills and suicide sprints. All it ever did was leave key players – especially those hit the most - like the star running backs and quarterbacks – injured on the sidelines by the time game day rolled around. Instead, Gagliardi instituted a "limited contact" practice, choosing instead to focus on the football fundamentals. He found that players in practice would often mentally focus on hitting as hard as possible or running as fast as they could, instead of focusing on form and technique – which in the long run, would make them better football players with more stamina when game time came around.

The 2008 and 2012 Republican primary seasons demonstrated the wisdom of Gagliardi's principles. Candidates used precious funding to "sack" each other, pushing in radical directions to differentiate themselves, and at the end of the day, distracting from the main show – winning the general election. Meanwhile, what were the Democrats doing? Consolidating, patiently laying groundwork, and winning.

The 2016 election poses the same threats if there isn't a change in approach. The GOP is currently a leaderless party, and the present number of politickers jumping on the Obama scandal bandwagon is a sign that it could be another crowded field. The drop in Obama's polling numbers is a huge opportunity for Republicans to renew their offensive. But the easiest way for GOP candidates to throw away this opportunity is to go on the offensive against each other. Spending months bludgeoning, outspending, and playing the "I can run further right than you can" game counts as throwing it all away.

There are two main problems contributing to the "full contact" GOP primary process. (There were three, but Ron Paul retired.) The first is that the barrier to entry into the race is far too low, bringing in those who are not in it to win it. On top of this, there is no real incentive to get out, as the era of chivalrous bowing out is dead. To the contrary, there are attractive incentives to stay in. Candidates, regardless of their qualifications or background, get significant, free media attention. Non-serious contenders enter to boost name recognition for future endeavors, grab book deals about their non-serious candidacy, or become regular Fox News commentators criticizing the GOP candidates for the rest of the election and beyond. As Jon Huntsman pointed out, "Some do it professionally. Some were entertainers. I looked down the debate stage, and half of them were probably on Fox contracts at one point in their career. You do that. You write some books. You go out and you sell some more. You get a radio gig or a TV gig out of it or something. And it's like, you say to yourself, the barriers of entry to this game are pretty damn low."[64]

The low barriers mean more amateurs looking for big hits and knockout blows. Long-shot candidates are incentivized to focus particularly on frontrunners. Again, Gagliardi's simple but game-winning question comes to mind. Why allow a process that puts your quarterbacks and running backs on injured reserve?

The second major problem is that there are too many TV debates. Debates are an important part of the process, and a good discussion on platform ideas and qualifications needs to be had. But not 20 of them. That's 20 opportunities for campaign-ending gaffes and GOP-tagging slip-ups. As RNC chair Reince Priebus lamented, "If you have 10 presidential candidates, and seven out of 10 or eight out of 10 will take whatever two-hour slot that is open to them, then you end up with a debate any time some network decides to hold one."[65]

Let me be clear. Debates are good. But these are not really debates. When Abraham Lincoln debated Frederick Douglas in Ottawa, Illinois, Douglas spoke for an hour. Then Lincoln spoke for an hour and a half. Then Douglas spoke for another half hour. *That* was a debate. But when a moderator asks nine motley panelists, who could include the likes of Tom Tancredo and Alan Keyes, to raise their hands if they believe in global warming, that is not a debate; it's a farce.

Not only are there too many debates, but they have also become episodes of political "Survivor," hijacked by the major networks but willingly agreed to by candidates seeking any TV time whatsoever. Debates no longer showcase candidates' strengths on substantive issues, but instead showcase who has mastered the "gotcha" question and who has done the most digging into the personal pasts of his fellow candidates. These so-called debates give the public a sustained and memorable look into the crazy uncles of the GOP.

The low barrier to entry, combined with two-hour "gotcha games," fosters the perfect situation for damaging, clownish behavior, not serious and sustained political discussion. Last year, by the time the general election campaign started, candidates who catapulted into the public arena through the debates were responsible for the following self-inflicted wounds to the Republican brand:

- **Michelle Bachmann**: Among her share of gaffes were ones that contributed to the GOP's image as the "anti-science party" – such as when she repeated the claim that HPV immunization can cause mental retardation – and to the GOP's fanaticism regarding ObamaCare – like when she said: "Let's repeal this failure before it literally kills women, kills children, kills senior citizens."[66]

- **Ron Paul:** Principled but impractical, Paul made the kinds of irrelevant, personal attacks we should expect only from Democrats, like calling Newt Gingrich a "chickenhawk."[67]

- **Herman Cain:** By the time Cain bowed out, he had alienated everyone from Hispanics (he suggested a moat between the United States and Mexico with alligators in it) to women (he had a Clintonian appetite for sexual harassment) to those who think the president should be able to find, or at least pronounce, Uzbekistan (which he proudly called "Ubeki-beki-beki-beki-stan-stan").[68][69]

- **Newt Gingrich:** Over the course of the final few debates, Gingrich led a Romney assault equivalent to a multi-day tackling drill. He was on the air presenting Romney as a liar, as a job-killing corporate raider, as an out-of-touch rich guy, as unprincipled, and at one point, as a friend to "radical … right wing social engineering."[70] And all from a candidate who was often said to have "more baggage than a Louis Vuitton factory."

- **Rick Perry:** I'm not sure who thought channeling the lesser qualities of President George W. Bush would make for a good candidate, but someone did and encouraged Perry to run. "OOPS." He helped preserve the worst impressions of the Republican Party left behind by Bush, when he forgot the few government agencies he would cut, and when he said Federal Reserve Chairman Ben Bernanke should face "Texas justice" for treason.[71]

- **Rick Santorum** – As an unlikely frontrunner, Santorum had plenty of time to represent the social conservative wing of the GOP in an election where jobs were foremost on voters' minds. But that didn't stop him from making time for Romney-damaging one-liners:

  o "I don't know of one group of people that's more disliked than politicians – it may be the folks who gave us the Wall Street bailout. And that's where Mitt Romney comes from."[72]

  o "It really has to do with what your principles and what your core is. I have a core … And that's a sharp contrast with Mitt Romney, who was for RomneyCare … This is someone who doesn't have a core. He's been on both sides of almost every single issue in the past 10 years."[73]

Rowdy crowds: GOP candidates weren't the only debate participants to raise questions about the electability of the GOP. The audience booed gay soldiers, applauded executions, and cheered about letting an uninsured patient die.

The "Law of Large Numbers" in politics says that the more times you speak, the more chances there are for errors, gaffes, and damaging 30-second sound bites. It works the same way as Gagliardi's "laws" – the more times someone is hit, the more chances there are for them to get injured. By the 14th debate – the first debate after the nominating contests officially kicked off – the credibility of the entire field had been damaged in some way.

So did the clown-car-rally-meets-demolition-derby primary season hurt Romney in the general election? Polling by Purple Strategies indicated that over the course of the campaign, Romney's unfavorablity increased by 18 points.[74] During the busy primary months of November-December 2011, a NBC/WSJ poll found that Romney's negative score "jumped to 42 percent with independents, his highest recorded negative rating in the poll with the crucial voting bloc."[75] Further, CBS news polling found Romney's January 2012 drop in support against the president "attributable to a shift among independents.[76] In other words, after a bruised and bloodied Mitt Romney limped to the nomination, independents were turned off by a candidate who appeared increasingly strident to win against his primary opponents.

Primary debates should be held purely to educate registered Republicans and right-leaning independents so they can make a more informed choice from real, credible candidates. They should not be for the network executives or for the Democratic-propaganda peddlers so that they can collect a treasure trove of "errant statements" and gaffes to use against the eventual Republican nominee once the general election kicks off.

So how to save the primary, and the GOP's general-election candidate, from another brutal beating? There is no "foolproof" way to go about it, but we can look to history. Some simple guidelines that would restore the integrity of the primary debates:

1. Take back debates from the network executives who don't have the GOP's interests at heart and have the RNC select the debate moderators.

2. Limit the period to six or seven primary debates, the same numbers that it respectively took in 1980 and 1988 to allow for open debate and lesser-known candidates to make their points.

3. Limit debate participation to those who have at least a five percent average in the national polls.

Taking back the White House involves taking back our own nomination process. And taking back the integrity of our nomination process involves looking to the "limited contact" rule. We can restore the GOP brand only if we put an end to the primary process madness and say goodbye to the negativity, to the gaffes, to the sideshows – and to George Stephanopoulos.

IT'S ALL ABOUT THE Q

In 2010, Joe Namath was declared one of the NFL's top 100 players of all time, with fans rating him #42.[77] While Namath certainly had moments of brilliance, a closer look at his statistics reveals him to be one of the most overrated quarterbacks of all time. Namath had significantly more interceptions than touchdown passes and didn't have a single touchdown in the heralded 1969 Super Bowl upset of the Baltimore Colts.[78] What made him one of the greatest NFL players of all time in the minds of his fans was his status as the NFL's first true media icon.

The night following the Jets' 1968 AFC title game victory, Joe Namath poured champagne over the head of TV-show host Johnny Carson. Perhaps not the best way to win friends among the media personalities of the day, but it was representative of his approach to making a name for himself in media. Namath was a minor actor in several movies, guest starred on a number of television shows, guest hosted the Tonight Show several times and was a color commentator for the NFL in later years.

"Broadway" Joe was affectionately remembered after one minor Broadway appearance. Republicans, on the other hand, seem only to get their nicknames from major gaffes (unless you consider "Etch-a-Sketch Mitt" or "Legitimate Rape" Akin affectionate nicknames.) There's a lesson for Republicans in Joe Namath. What Broadway Joe did is true not only in sports, but also in politics. If the GOP can better manage its cultural image by improving its media favorability and access, then people will look beyond the records and results of past failures that are holding it back.

On January 31, 2009, President Obama delivered his weekly radio address from the White House – a tradition that started with Franklin D. Roosevelt but did not become regularized until 1982 by President Reagan. President Obama's address was a dramatic departure from those of his predecessors. Why? Because the President was the first to video his radio addresses. Television broadcasts have existed since 1929. Why was Barack Obama the first guy to figure out that just as many people might watch his weekly addresses as would listen to him on the radio? Or that his videotaped address might also be replayed on cable news programs?

The answer is obvious and also a little sad. Obama understands the television age in ways that most Republicans still do not. It's a little worse than that, actually. Republicans mock Obama for his television and cultural savvy rather than trying to learn from him.

The GOP similarly scoffed when, in February of 2013, Michelle Obama became the first First Lady to present an Academy Award via satellite from the White House. Her appearance – which lasted all of two minutes – was watched by 40.3 million people around the world and contributed to 2.1 million tweets.[79] Think Mitch McConnell gets those kinds of ratings for his umpteenth appearance on "Face the Nation" or Charlie Rose?

In 2012, the Obamas surpassed Ronald and Nancy Reagan in combined TV and movie appearances (195 to date versus the Reagans' lifetime 175 appearances.)[80] And they are on a path to pass over 20 years of appearances by media-obsessive Bill and Hillary Clinton by the end of Obama's term.

What President Obama has learned at the expense of the GOP is Rule #7: Reaching out to a wide variety of television shows, magazines, cable channels, and publications (essentially more than just Fox News) means reaching more of the electorate and becoming a familiar presence in their homes.

Ever heard of the Q score? It's not quite the equivalent of Rasmussen polling or RealClearPolitics averages. A Q score identifies the familiarity of a person or brand and their appeal for those that are familiar. It is used for any range of celebrities, musicians, artists, and politicians to measure likeability and connectedness. The Q score is calculated by dividing the percentage of those who respond "very" favorably to the subject person or brand by the percentage of those who are familiar with that person or brand. So, say, if 10 percent of people respond favorably to Snooki and 75 percent of people know who she is, she gets a positive Q score of 13. Those in the media and entertainment industries live and die by their Q ratings – a score near 50 is considered phenomenal. Here are the current leaders in terms of likeability in American culture today[81]:

- Tom Hanks (50)
- Morgan Freeman (50)
- Clint Eastwood (46)
- Bill Cosby (43)

These celebrities have carefully cultivated friendly, non-threatening images in a variety of mediums. That's also what smart politicians like Obama are doing today. They appear on outlets as diverse in substance as C-SPAN and ESPN. While voters may become familiar with political headlines and personalities, they know next to nothing about the substance of the issues. Having a strong "cultural" image or perception can be far more effective than any well-articulated policy position. The shift in cable news to "opinion"-based reporting over straight fact-based reporting contributes to the problem of trying to get a policy across versus a general impression. If voters think they are familiar with a candidate or party brand, they won't need to go any farther into actual substance and policies before making a judgment.

President Obama does not take time out of his busy day of covering up scandals to show up on The View with the goal of winning over conservative voters. He is not on Jay Leno to "reach across the aisle." He's there to simply be in the spotlight, show that he's an average hard-working American who's susceptible to humor every once in a while and not about to keel over into his grave, like far too many GOP candidates. Ask Obama a question about Lady Gaga and you're not going to get a blank stare. Ask Obama about NBA star Lebron James, and you're not going to get an awkward, fumbling response.

Candidates can fight the policy battles to their hearts' content on political talk shows, but if the GOP doesn't fight for its day in the sun in pop culture, we're going to see even grimmer results on Election Day.

So how should the GOP approach this branding problem? Well for one, they have to understand that we live in what I like to call a "TMZ/ESPN society." We live in a pop culture-crazed, sports-obsessed culture. While news networks capture the attention of fewer than 10 percent of voters, Letterman, Saturday Night Live and major sporting events take up the majority of Americans' couch-potato time – especially self-described moderates and young voters.[82]

At one time, being seen as a celebrity posed an obstacle to the politically-minded. Just ask Ronald Reagan and Arnold Schwarzenegger, who overcame significant doubts about their Hollywood personalities to get to elected office. No longer. That time has clearly passed; to everyone except John McCain that is. No anecdote more clearly demonstrates being out of touch than the McCain campaign's ad attacking

Obama for his "celebrity" status. The idea that Obama's "celebrity" status would be disagreeable to the majority of Americans ironically demonstrates the GOP's ignorance. They're out of touch with the out of touch.

Saddled with a weak economy and fighting a relatively difficult re-election battle, Obama's campaign decided to avoid the White House Press Corps and take another path, launching a paradoxically heavy soft-media strategy.[83] On outlets ranging from ESPN to Entertainment Tonight to People magazine, Obama talked sports, workout songs, and local restaurants, not local government, national obesity, and malnutrition. In a nutshell, the Obama campaign wisely understood that as bad as things were, few Americans were actually paying attention to politics.

Appearing on The View or filling out an NCAA bracket for ESPN can be just as useful, if not more so, to maintaining a favorable public opinion rating, even if the cost is upsetting a few Duke Blue Devils fans.

Here are four rules that should be plastered on the walls of the RNC and Capitol Hill Club.

1. Pay attention to ratings and audiences. Become conversant with popular shows and celebrities. A glance at ratings of various shows and events tends to put things into perspective, especially in a town where all the effort is put on getting a hit on CNN during the day or a spot on one of the Sunday news shows.

For example, here are some typical viewer numbers for various programs[84]:

- The Super Bowl – 108.4 million
- The Oscars (2013) – 40.3 million
- American Idol Finale – 14.3 million
- Dancing with the Stars Finale – 13.8 million
- Wheel of Fortune – 10.5 million
- Judge Judy (syndicated) – 9 million
- Jeopardy – 8.9 million
- 60 Minutes – 8.7 million
- World News Tonight (ABC) – 7.1 million
- Big Bang Theory – 6.4 million
- America's Funniest Home Videos (Rerun) – 5 million
- Entertainment Tonight – 4.9 million
- Pawn Stars – 4.78 million
- WWE Wrestling – 4.3 million
- Inside Edition – 4.2 million
- Game of Thrones Finale (HBO) – 4-5 million
- Dr. Phil – 3.8 million
- American Pickers – 3.63 million
- Dr. Oz – 3.4 million
- The View – 3-4 million
- SpongeBob Square Pants – 2.85 million
- Face the Nation – 2.8 million
- Live with Kelly and Michael (yes, Strahan) – 2.6 million

- Ellen DeGeneres (syndicated) – 2.5 million
- Katie Couric (syndicated) – 2.5 million
- Hannity – 2.4 million
- Dallas (TNT) – 2.4 million
- Meet the Press – 2.3 million
- Charlie Rose – 2 million
- Daily Show (Comedy) – 1.9 million
- Colbert Report (Comedy) – 1.5 million
- Seinfeld (re-run, TBS) – 1.45 million
- Fox and Friends—1.123 million
- Real Housewvies of Beverly Hills (Bravo) – 1.1 million
- Anderson Cooper – 567,000

The chart is interesting. Ten times as many people watch a rerun of America's Funniest Home Videos, for example, than Anderson Cooper's program on CNN. That doesn't mean politicians should start making their own goofy videos, but they should be aware that there are many, many programs out there that far and away exceed the reach and viewership of the Beltway staples.

2. Engage non-Washington media. The RNC should engage the ever-expanding media that the average American absorbs on an everyday basis, and use the media to reach people who are not found on their couch during the Sunday morning talk shows. Establishing the faces of the Republican Party does

not require a press conference but simply a late-night show appearance, showing up at a major sporting event, or having the ability to make fun of yourself every once in a while.

3. <u>Talk about something other than politics</u>. The American people want their elected representatives to be like them – or at least seem like them. Most politicians aren't. They're ambitious, borderline-sociopathic creatures who have few interests outside furthering their political careers. They don't bother watching SportsCenter because they're too busy watching Morning Joe or reading *The Washington Post* editorial page. But politicians need to at least feign interest in pop culture. When Marco Rubio talks about the Miami rap scene and his friendship with Pitbull, he gets credibility points. When former Indiana Governor Mitch Daniels starts talking about his love of Harley Davidsons, he seems more likable.

There are some on the Republican side who get this. New Jersey Governor Chris Christie seems to be someone who gets modern American interests. From his almost stalker-status Bruce Springsteen reverence to his self-aiming humor on Saturday Night Live and David Letterman, Christie has positioned himself in the mindset of the American public for more than just his policies.[85] Touring Hurricane Sandy damage with the President and simply shaking his hand on national television can go a long way toward fulfilling the American voters' desire for some semblance of bipartisanship more so than co-signing a low-key agricultural bill that gets a few views on C-SPAN. When the average voter would prefer to have a beer with the GOP candidate than the Democratic one, we're on the right track.

Americans are not always electing the most competent person of the two to be president, but someone they feel comfortable with leading the nation. In many ways, we are no longer electing the leader of the free world, but America's "class president."

We don't have Q scores for politicians. But it's hard to imagine Barack Obama's is lower than those of the Republicans leadership – the bland and dour twosome of Mitch McConnell and John Boehner. The two men don't exactly ooze sex appeal. *The Washington Post* reported in April that only 23 percent of Americans believe the GOP is "in touch with the concerns of most people in the United States today," while 70 percent believe that it is "out of touch."[86] It doesn't matter if the GOP can talk about how their policies better address the concerns and needs of the American people during the McLaughlin Group if they can't break into society's TMZ/ESPN mindset.

2016 will present a chance to put the McCain and Romney days behind the GOP. As Broadway Joe demonstrated, it doesn't take a stellar track record to be remembered and revered. The Democratic Party understands this. Hillary Clinton is slated to have both a book and a movie on her life released by 2016. She has been named Gallup's most admired woman 17 times, while one of America's least favorite women, Paris Hilton, is more popular than the current Republican-controlled Congress.[87] It's time that the GOP add Q scores to the electoral indicators they follow.

RULE #8

NEVER UNDERESTIMATE VOTER IGNORANCE ... AND INDIFFERENCE

Are you still talking about the maneuverings last week by the guests on "Meet the Press"? Did you enjoy the latest debate over cloture on an amendment to an appropriations bill on C-SPAN? If you answered yes to these questions, you probably live in Washington, D.C. Or you are a shut-in. You are almost certainly not a "regular" American, most of whom couldn't care less about all the goings on in the nation's capital, which they find a baffling, useless, wasteful mess. I'd wager the vast majority don't even know what day or time they could find "Meet the Press" on their TV sets. They are probably in church.

American voters are not stupid, but when it comes to Washington, it might be said they suffer from severe "Attention Deficit Disorder." They don't need or want to be lectured on the coming debt crisis. They aren't particularly sure what a "fiscal cliff" or "sequestration" is. They know they probably should care about such things, but their minds tend to wander when people start to explain it. Can anyone blame them? They just need to hear that America is spending more money than it has. They'll figure out the rest.

As a whole, Americans are ignorant about politics. It's a strong statement, but it's true. They lack even a basic understanding of the intricacies of the legislative process, and little has inspired them to bother to correct that. They know little about the origins of the Democratic or Republican parties, or what truly differentiates them. They have jobs. They have their kids' soccer games. They have their families. And they have entertainment from films, the Internet, and TV. Washington, by contrast, is boring.

In 2006, veteran political pollster John Zogby found that nearly three-quarters of those asked could name each of the Three Stooges – Larry, Curly and Moe – but only 42 percent were able to identify the three branches of the federal government (the legislative, executive and judicial.) Even Senator Charles Schumer, a Democrat, missed that one, once labeling the three branches of government as "the House, the Senate, and the President."[88] Zogby's survey also found that 77 percent of Americans could name two of the Seven Dwarfs from the Disney blockbuster *Snow White*. Just 24 percent could name at least two of the nine Supreme Court Justices. [89]

Things have not gotten any better since that survey was conducted. In early 2010 – when ObamaCare was passed by Congress into law – a Pew Research survey found that only a quarter (26 percent) of Americans knew that it takes 60 votes to break a filibuster in the U.S. Senate and force a vote on a bill.[90] In the summer of 2012, Pew found that just 40 percent could correctly state that the Republican Party held a majority of the seats in the U.S. House of Representatives.[91]

What about our youth, the bright and inspiring minds that can look forward to digging their way out of the mountain of debt the president has accumulated? The results are in, and when it comes to younger Americans, their general knowledge of politics, and basic geography, is beyond alarming. According to a National Geographic survey, "[h]alf or fewer of young men and women 18-24 can identify the states of New York or Ohio on a map (50% and 43%, respectively)."[92] According to National Geographic, when confronted with their lack of knowledge, many young Americans did not seem to be "particularly alarmed."

This puts Washington's leaders at an obvious disadvantage, since they are experts in something no sane person outside of Washington cares about, sort of like being a specialist in the manufacturing of rubber bands or butter. That means that current and aspiring officeholders need to reach the voters through charm and wit – qualities that are especially lacking among the gray, old, and decidedly untrendy leaders of the GOP.

History has shown time and again that leaders best able to relate to the American people on their terms – as the pollsters say, the kind of person you'd like to have a beer with – tend to win elections. Dwight Eisenhower was more likable and relatable than Adlai Stevenson, John F. Kennedy more than Nixon, Reagan more than Carter, H.W. Bush more than Dukakis, Clinton more than H.W. Bush and Bob Dole (who was often referred to as "Darth Vader").[93] George W. Bush seemed more in touch with people than either of his opponents, Al Gore or John Kerry, and Barack Obama of course was more relatable than McCain and Romney. This was no small feat for Obama – a Harvard-trained elitist professor with an unusual name and a temperature best described as lukewarm – who somehow managed to seem more down to earth than all of his opponents combined.

Though it wasn't always the case – see the aforementioned Dukakis, Kerry and Gore – Democrats seem to have a better handle on how to excite the pulse rate of the voters and at the very least gain their attention. Their leaders tend to appear on television programs that have high ratings – "The View," "Late Show with David Letterman," "The Daily Show," for example. They talk in emotional terms to voters about issues that can be quickly and easily understood.

Unfortunately for the GOP, today's political errors don't include the routine backdoor dealings of the Democratic Party such as the Cornhusker Kickback and the Louisiana Purchase (the cushy earmarks doled out to Senators Ben Nelson and Mary Landrieu in return for their aye votes on ObamaCare), or the daily lies in economic statistics and budget data that look far worse than a "pig with makeup," or gun-running across our borders done by our own federal law enforcement agencies. No, political errors today are measured in gaffes, the snippets that the drive-by media can pick up, zip down the street, and drop at the doorstep of your laptop in seconds. If Buzzfeed has a .gif of your gaffe, that's going to have far more of an impact than any policy address or substance.

When the GOP has tried to get down to the basics, it has fumbled, both literally and figuratively. In 2012 Newt Gingrich labeled Paul Ryan's Medicare plan – a plan few across the country knew about or understood – as "radical." That "gaffe" and the fight among Republicans became a far more interesting discussion than the substance of the bill. And let's not forget the time Senate candidate Todd Akin tried to explain how babies are made. Republicans in fact have a bizarre fixation with talking about "rape." Back in 1990, a Texas businessman named Clayton Williams was leading the polls to be governor of the state, when he casually made a joke about rape. "If it's inevitable," he said, "just relax and enjoy it."[94] Folks in Texas could spot a loser and offensive boor from a mile off. They ended up supporting Democrat Ann Richards in droves.

The last two GOP presidential cycles have presented more than enough comedy to fuel Saturday Night Live, the Colbert Report, and too many Daily Shows, in large part because of the Republicans' one big mistake: Assuming that the electorate both knows and cares about complex legislative policies more than it actually does. Indifference on the part of most voters only turned into interest with each and every one of Romney's stumbles. "Binders full of women" quickly became binders full of incensed voters, especially young voters. Voters didn't give a fig about Romney's 59-point plan to turn around the economy. They did care that he was a totally unrelatable automaton who belonged to a religion he seemed uncomfortable talking about.

The revolutionary football coach Paul Brown said, "Football is a game of errors. The team that makes the fewest errors in a game usually wins." If the GOP wants to be the party that represents America, then it should heed the words that dictate America's favorite sport. Those who think that the GOP needs to innovate, reinvent the wheel, and develop a new West Coast offense are missing the point. It's much easier – and oddly enough much harder – than that. The famous acronym is KISS: Keep it simple, stupid.

1. Remember the world outside Rush and Fox News. Talking to the base is easy and comfortable. But it is also limited. There's a larger group of people who are interested in conservative ideas but don't stay glued to Hannity on the Fox News Channel or catch Mark Levin every night. Republicans need to be prepared and ready to go to other media outlets – in this day and age there are literally hundreds out there – to reach people who have only heard from Democrats and hosts sympathetic to them.

If you think going on C-SPAN accomplishes this, you are wrong. Remember the old riddle, "If a tree falls in a forest and no one is there to hear it, does it make a sound?" Well, here's the Washington variant of that. "If you appear on C-SPAN and nobody outside your office sees it, did anyone hear you?" Answer: No. I'm talking about "The View" and "The Talk" – if you haven't heard of both of those shows, that's part of the problem – as well as countless magazines that reach real people like, for example, People. There are women's magazines and men's magazines, hunting and fishing publications, and any number of websites that cater to a wide range of viewpoints and interests. Republicans should pick their top 10 communicators – if there are that many – and disperse them to the winds, where they can define the party's beliefs, correct inaccuracies, and agree to disagree on various issues. Staying insulated in today's media world is deadly.

2. <u>Try to speak like you are talking to a friend or relative</u>. In the normal world, you wouldn't talk to people like you are Bob Dole, the legislative master who knew so many tricks, maneuvers and congressional shorthand terms that he couldn't seem to communicate to normal people. Dole would say things like, "We've got something in markup on that" and people would scratch their heads. Think about the political mileage Obama gets out of catchphrases and open-ended language like "fair share," "balanced approach," "common sense" proposals. These are open-ended, vague terms, but the GOP has no counters to them. Which brings us to another important rule.

3. <u>Banish the following words/phrases from Republican officeholders' vocabulary immediately</u>:

- Markup
- Quorum call
- Sequester
- Rescission
- Filibuster (some people might know this one, but better safe than sorry)
- Appropriation (try "spending bill" instead)
- Conference agreement/ Conference report
- Fiscal year
- Earmark
- Carve outs/Set asides
- Entitlements (say "Social Security" and "Medicare")
- The Beltway (most people outside of it don't use the phrase)
- GDP or GNP
- C-SPAN
- Legislative Rider
- Supermajority
- Legislation (try "law" or "bill" or "proposal")
- "The Cornhusker Kickback" or "The Louisiana Purchase" (no one outside Washington knows what this refers to)
- Almost all acronyms, other than those that are commonly understood (CIA, FBI, IRS)
- Rape, "legitimate" or otherwise.
- Television shows that aired before 1980 (not to pick on Bob Dole again, but in his 1996 campaign he once faked a heart attack before a baffled crowd to mimic a character on "Sanford and Son.")

4. <u>Listen to what you are saying as you say it</u>. Think about the damage that ill-considered language has done to GOP candidates. Sorry boys, but "legitimate rape," "the 47 percent," "Let Detroit go bankrupt," "I like to fire people," and "Corporations are people" are disastrous for the GOP brand. Watching your language doesn't make you "a hack."[95] In fact playing good defense on the basketball court involves very little hacking. It also doesn't mean holding back on the truth, like that a $16 trillion debt is unsustainable. But it does mean that defining a public image is important. Saying "no" consistently is not a good public image.

Watching your language also doesn't mean giving up your principles. The American people like principles, so it's time that the GOP started speaking to the public as if they had them, with clear phrases that convey those principles. The Democratic Party seems to have no problem doing so. When they frame the debate around principles of universal healthcare, the social safety net, and asking the wealthy to pay just a tiny bit more (What's a couple million dollars more? It's all relative.), they win the battle outright.

In short, the Republicans need to rethink completely their communications strategy. The first step in that is understanding their audience better. As the joke goes, "Half of the American people have never read a newspaper. Half never voted for President. One hopes it is the same half." Unfortunately, it often isn't.

RULE #9

THE PRESEASON DOESN'T WIN YOU THE SUPER BOWL

In August 2008, the Detroit Lions moonwalked through their four preseason games, winning every one by an average of 12 points. This was the anemic Detroit Lions, long one of the worst teams in the NFL, a team so bad that people felt sorry for their fans. The 4-0 preseason record shocked fans and pundits alike, leading to all sorts of optimistic predictions about the Lions' future. The Detroit Lions, of all teams, were no longer the bottom feeders of professional sports. By season's end, the Lions did make history alright, but not as the pundits predicted (and fans hoped). They became the first team in National Football League history to complete the beautiful disaster of a 0-16 record.

The bottom line is that winning in the "preseason" might be a reason for hope, but it not a reason to jump to conclusions. By the end of the 2014 elections, let's hope the

GOP is not in the same boat – that is, feeling triumphant in off-year elections and deciding that means they're ready for 2016 and the Super Bowl.

It is never wise to make ballot box predictions more than one year out, or in the case of the legendary 1948 Dewey versus Truman campaign, a few hours out. But it is probably safe to say that Election Day 2014 *should* on balance prove fruitful for the Republican Party, despite the toxic nature of the GOP brand. And if the GOP doesn't make significant gains in 2014, the party will be in a worse downward spiral than even the most pessimistic among us might have thought.

The reasons for Republican optimism are many. Midterm elections are generally skewed against the party in power in the White House. Since 1866, the incumbent's party has lost ground in 35 of 38 midterms.[96] Bill Clinton is the only president in the last century whose party has gained congressional seats in his second midterm, and even then the GOP retained a majority in the House.

The average voter turnout rate falls for midterms, from an average 63 percent turnout in presidential election years to 48 percent in non-presidential elections.[97] The expected lower turnout for the midterms generally means an older, whiter, more affluent electorate. Seniors are an incredibly reliable voting bloc in midterm years, and their role in previous elections means that the senior constituency will be crucial in the 2014 election. That doesn't bode well for the Democrats. President Obama lost the senior vote in 2008 and again in 2012, that time by 12 points.[98] No matter how many times the Obama folks rolled out campaign ads with Paul Ryan look-alikes pushing old granny off the cliff in a wheelchair, America's senior citizens didn't vote for him. And soon-to-be senior citizens – voters ages 50 to 64 – will also be key. Obama lost their vote in 2012 by five points, even though he had won a majority of that demographic in 2008.[99]

Young voters – ages 19 to 29 – are unlikely to fill the gap. In the 2010 midterms they represented a meager 12 percent of the overall vote versus 19 percent in 2012. The electorate's racial composition also differs between presidential and off-year elections. Fewer African-American and Latino voters made it to the polls in 2010, with African-Americans falling from 13 percent to 11 percent and Latinos from 10 percent to eight percent.[100][101]

In addition to the demographic challenges confronting the Democrats, the individual open seats are especially problematic for them. Here's a quick rundown:

Senate Races 2014:

In the upper house of the U.S. legislative branch, Democrats currently have a lead of 54-46, meaning that the GOP needs to pick up six seats to win an outright majority. Vice President Biden casts the deciding vote in the case of a 50-50 deadlock and Republicans will almost certainly lose the New Jersey Senate special election in 2013.

Several stars have aligned for the GOP to make solid gains. Of the 35 seats up for election, 20 are currently controlled by Democrats, putting the Democrats in a defensive position as they try to hold on.[102] The Republican opportunities are enhanced by the retirement of reasonably popular incumbents in Iowa (Tom Harkin), Montana (Max Baucus), South Dakota (Tim Johnson), Michigan (Carl Levin) and West Virginia (Jay Rockefeller). A number of the other seats include Democratic incumbents in states where Romney defeated Obama in 2012 (Mary Landrieu in Louisiana, Mark Pryor in Arkansas, Mark Begich in Alaska, and Kay Hagan in North Carolina). Republicans, by contrast, have far fewer vulnerable seats to defend with the most vulnerable being Kentucky (McConnell) and Georgia (open).

I agree with political prognosticator Charlie Cook. The most likely path to a GOP Senate majority means picking up the open seats in West Virginia, South Dakota and Montana, while simultaneously working to defeat the vulnerable incumbents in Arkansas, Louisiana, North Carolina and Alaska; while holding Kentucky and Georgia.[103] That is not to say that other paths to the majority won't open up. As political stats guru Nate Silver notes, depending on what transpires over the next year, Republicans could improve their chances at picking up other open seats, namely Michigan and Iowa.[104]

Current Senate Minority Leader Mitch McConnell has made no secret of his desire to serve as the body's Majority Leader. If it doesn't come to pass in 2014, it's a reasonably safe supposition that it won't happen while McConnell resides in the Senate. And as long as the GOP manages to nominate statewide candidates who can competently string together a few words into a sentence and manage to avoid the duds who feel obliged to offer up their opinions on what constitutes "legitimate rape," there is an outside chance the Senate gavel could be resting in McConnell's hand come January 2015.

House Races 2014:

Republicans will go into the 2014 midterm election with 234 seats to Democrats' 201 seats. This means that Democrats would need to net at least 17 seats to regain control of the House in 2014 and re-install Nancy Pelosi as Speaker. According to political handicapper Stuart Rothenberg, only four House races are considered "pure toss-ups," part of 47 seats that are "in play."[105] To achieve a 218-seat majority in the House, Democrats would essentially need to outperform the GOP by 10 points nationally on the generic ballot.[106] Current polling places Democrats at a few points ahead on the generic ballot. The Cook Political Report 2014 Partisan Voter Index puts it in clearer terms, stating that: "Democrats would need to hold all Democratic-leaning seats and win 30 Republican-leaning seats to win a majority."[107] What's the bottom line? When the smoke clears after Election Day 2014, the GOP will remain in control of the U.S. House of Representatives. Yards could be gained on either side, but the ball is not close enough to the 50-yard line for a surprise swing to occur.

Gubernatorial Races 2014 (& 2013):

The GOP currently controls 30 of the 50 governors' mansions, and will likely retain a majority (albeit smaller) after 2014. There are three reasons why the GOP should be safe at the state level: 1) Americans have a more favorable view of their state government than the federal government, making turnover less likely; 2) GOP governors are given more leeway to run independently of the party brand and to market themselves on their own terms, even though shots at the Obama administration will still be common; 3) All but nine of the 48 governors with four-year terms are elected in an off-year, when the presidential race is not at the top of the ticket, giving the GOP the same advantages it historically has for midterm elections.[108]

In short, barring a major scandal or absolute catastrophe, Republicans should enter the year 2015 with more seats in the Senate, a majority in the House and a majority of governorships in the nation. That's not much different from where the GOP is today.

Media will make much ado about the 2014 elections — the stakes and consequences — because that sort of hype drives ratings and gets attention. But as two well-respected political observers wrote in August of 2010, the truth is that "midterm elections are largely determined by short-term factors, including the popularity of the president and the state of the economy. As a result, they rarely indicate anything about longer-term trends, and they have no value in predicting the results of the subsequent presidential and congressional elections."

"Presidents whose parties have suffered major midterm losses — such as Harry Truman in 1946, Ronald Reagan in

1982 and Bill Clinton in 1994 – have gone on to win re-election easily two years later. So even if Republicans make major gains in 2010, as is widely expected, it won't tell us anything about what will happen in 2012."[109] That, of course, turned out to be true.

I have this recurring nightmare that on the day after the 2014 midterm election, I am going to turn on the radio or the TV after Republicans have a relatively good night and the conservative chattering class is going to declare that the GOP is back from the dead. They will pronounce that people like me, who argue that the GOP needs to make some drastic changes, were full of malarkey, and that all the party needed to do was double down on its conservative ideology. Trust me, that nightmare is going to come true.

On December 28, 2008, an announcer for the Detroit Lions Radio network counted down the last seconds of the Lion's final game that season, against the Green Bay Packers. "The Lions find themselves in a very familiar position," he said. "For 16 weeks, starting in Atlanta back in September, they took the field thinking this was gonna be their day. Sixteen times they were wrong, and now there are no Sundays left."[110] Without radical changes to the GOP, a commentator will be saying something similar in the aftermath of the 2016 elections – the third presidential election in a row in which the GOP ended up a loser, no matter how promising they seemed to play in the preseasons.

RULE #10:

"THE 47 PERCENT" – NOT JUST A GAFFE, A PREDICTION

The Alabama Crimson Tide went into the 1970 season opener against the University of Southern California Trojans coming off of an embarrassing 6-5 season for the "flagship" team of southern college football. Legendary coach Paul "Bear" Bryant had led the Crimson Tide to three national championships in the 1960s, but those days were fading. Many wondered if it was time for Bryant to hang it up. Sophomore Sam Cunningham, a black fullback for USC, led the Trojans to rout the Crimson Tide 42-21 in a game evoking pain and helplessness in the collective memories of Alabama fans. Cunningham, who hadn't even expected to suit up that night, was USC coach John McKay's secret weapon in catching the Crimson Tide off guard; so much that historians have concluded that the notoriously obstinate Alabama fans and coaches didn't just accept the idea of integrating their team, but that they needed it after seeing Sam Cunningham score touchdown after touchdown in that drubbing. Cunningham is famously said to have done more to integrate Alabama in 60 minutes than Martin Luther King Jr. did in 20 years.[111]

How many election night beatings does the Republican Party need to take before they do more than accept and recognize the immense possibility of not only losing the popular vote for good, but also losing any path to the White House in the Electoral College? It is high time the Republican Party takes note of why it continues to lose.

"There are 47 percent of the people who will vote for the president no matter what," Mitt Romney confided to a group of wealthy donors in May of 2012. "There are 47 percent who are with him, who are dependent upon government, who believe that they are victims, who believe the government has a responsibility to care for them. Who believe that they are entitled to health care, to food, to housing, to you-name-it – that that's an entitlement. And the government should give it to them. And they will vote for this president no matter what. ... These are people who pay no income tax. ... [M]y job is not to worry about those people. I'll never convince them they should take personal responsibility and care for their lives."[112] Romney never intended for those comments to become public, but they did and they were widely criticized for writing off millions of Americans whose votes he needed to win. As inelegant as they were, there was truth in Romney's comments about the near hopelessness of his cause, but for totally different reasons. Republicans are going to have a hard time winning national elections, but it isn't because we have a nation of parasites dependent on government handouts. It's because demographics have made the electoral math nearly impossible for Republicans to win a national election.

If a strategy leads to embarrassing losses season after season, fans and owners mutually call for more than in-game substitutions or in-season roster changes. Players, coaches, or entire teams are sent packing to rebuild franchises from the ground up. Why then, has the GOP failed to take notice of its supporters essentially wearing paper bags over their heads as if they were fans for the 0-16 Detroit Lions back in 2008? A quarterback might be the reason for a bad season, like Mitt Romney in the 2012 election. That's not an excuse for a "franchise" that has lost five of the last six popular presidential votes. If, as Republican strategist Mike Murphy notes, Republicans need "the equivalent of drawing an inside straight in poker to get to the White House" there needs to be a fundamental reassessment of where things stand.[113]

Consider these numbers:
California (55)
Connecticut (7)
Delaware (3)
District of Columbia (3)
Hawaii (4)
Illinois (20)
Maine (4)

Maryland (10)
Massachusetts (11)
Michigan (16)
Minnesota (10)
New Jersey (14)
New Mexico (5)
New York (29)
Oregon (7)
Pennsylvania (20)
Rhode Island (4)
Vermont (3)
Washington (12)
Wisconsin (10)

These 19 states and the District of Columbia with 247 electoral votes are a virtual lock for the Democratic Party. That means in any election the Democratic candidate only needs 23 more electoral votes to win the presidency. They can do this with increasing ease, especially when you consider the states President Obama won in 2012. Florida alone would give them 29 electoral votes and a victory. Then there's Virginia, which Obama won twice, with 13 electoral votes, or North Carolina, which Obama won in 2008 but narrowly lost in 2012 with 15 electoral votes, and New Hampshire, with four, or Nevada with six, and Arizona with 11.

Former *New York Times* number-cruncher Nate Silver identifies that a large number of electorally critical states – such as Iowa, Nevada, Pennsylvania and Colorado – have been Democratic-leaning in the past two elections, driven by demographic shifts.[114] If the GOP won the popular vote by a reasonable margin, these states would likely turn red, but in a close election, it seems they are becoming consistently blue. Hoping for a transformation candidate to break through and win the popular vote outright, which will undoubtedly require reaching beyond the traditional GOP voting bloc, does not bode well for the future of the Republican Party.

Democrats have been working to expand their electoral map, while Republicans haven't done anything with theirs. When Obama showed up on the national scene in 2008, his campaign team worked assiduously to put states like Indiana, North Carolina and Virginia in play. These states used to be reliably Republican and now have tilted because Democratic politicians organized themselves for the long term.

And they have more ambitious plans in the future. Democrats have a Texas effort underway centered on Hispanics designed to take the perennial red state into swing state territory. This would all but guarantee that the Republicans never again win a national ticket.

Republicans have not had any success expanding the map in decades. They've tried feeble efforts in California and ended up with candidates who were pale echoes of Democrats and a Hollywood governor more suited to procreating with his housekeeper than offering a compelling Republican agenda for the state.

The unequivocal electoral math hasn't stopped some GOP strategists and pundits from dashing toward the bunker. They prefer to focus on the "Obama effect" – the electoral juggernaut of a once-in-a-generation politician whose rhetorical and political gifts and lock on minority voters make him unbeatable. They say Republicans can hunker down and count on their age-old (literally) strategy by recapturing the white vote. As ESPN college football analyst Lee Corso might say: "Not so fast, my friend."

Refocusing on the traditional white GOP base might make sense if all that was needed was a stronger candidate and better mobilization. But the white vote itself is fundamentally shifting. First, the percentage of white voting Americans is shrinking. In 2012, Romney lost when Caucasian Americans made up 63 percent of the population and 72 percent of voters.[115] Contrast this with the Census Bureau's estimates that by 2060, Caucasian Americans will be just 43 percent of the U.S. population.[116] In addition to the demographic shift, the white vote is shifting left. While white voters still show great concern for reckless spending and a dislike of raising of taxes, social issues are driving the GOP's base towards other options as traditional marriage declines, support for same-sex marriage has become a majority opinion, and the "nones" – people identifying as spiritual but not with an organized religion – continue to increase in population share.

In order for Republicans to win back the White House, keeping with the same stale strategy requires a terrible Democratic standard bearer (Think, Michael Dukakis and John Kerry) coupled with low minority vote turnouts. And even then the GOP might still need a friendly secretary of state in the most contested state. Any political strategy that relies on the opposition not showing up is no strategy at all; it's false hope.

"Bear" Bryant recognized he had to make a fundamental change. It's time Republicans stop digging into a deeper and deeper hole and take a fresh look at the American population they are seeking to represent. The temptation to blame bad candidates or the tea party or improved voter mobilization by the Democrats or any number of other excuses is a mistake. Winning the White House is not about appealing to groups per say. It is clear that it will take far more than winning over more Hispanic or youth votes for the GOP to turn itself around, because the white vote itself is shifting. It's about articulating a message that captures the imagination of broad sections of Americans. The biggest problem is staring the Republicans in the mirror – the appeal of the GOP brand, its message and to whom we reach out.

The point is that things are grim for the GOP. And even more so absent some fundamental changes in thinking and messaging. And it isn't going back on the values that define modern conservatism. Bear Bryant didn't release his entire team and only recruit black football players; he simply recognized the need for a fundamental shift.

Republicans need to demonstrate that they understand and care about the needs of average Americans, who are not at all convinced the current party in power has a lock on the answers. The fact that the Left can condemn a mainstream

for "waging a war on women" means that the
ng from a branding issue. Republicans must
make the point that their policies empower women and
give them a chance to succeed through their own initiative;
Democrats treat them as helpless wards of the state, made
clear in the frightening "Life of Julia" campaign promotion. On climate policy, the United States leads the world
since 2006 in emissions reduction thanks to programs
Republicans favor, such as the promotion of natural gas, and
not Democratic policies, such as the promotion of alternative
energy.[117]

One of the most storied teams in college football and
its coach could have ignored the fact that desegregation had
come to America – and its competitors. They could have continued to discriminate against qualified black football players – something that was not only morally repugnant, but
also mindless if the goal was to recruit the best and win.
But Bryant's career wasn't over. In 1971, he recruited black
players for the team. (By 1973, one-third of Alabama's start-
ers were black.)[118] He tossed the old power offense and put
in a new wishbone formation. The team had undergone a
remarkable turnaround to have an undefeated season in 1971.
Two years later, it would win another national title under
Bryant. The crusty old coach with the trademark, check-
ered fedora wouldn't let his team vanish into obscurity –
at least under his watch. If only the GOP could find a Bear
Bryant of its own.

2016 REPUBLICAN PRESIDENTIAL SCOUTING REPORT

More than three years out and the most wide-open field in recent memory is beginning to take shape. There is no clear pick to take the field in the 2016 season, someone who can carry the ball to the end zone without fumbling along the way. 2012 was not kind to the also-rans, so there are no prohibitive front-runners, making for another interesting race for the ages.

Republicans would be wise to run their own primary and not pay too much attention to "Hillary mania" (that doesn't mean say anything you want on the stump because 20 minutes after the 2014 midterms conclude, Hillary mania will likely kick into overdrive), and select a candidate they feel comfortable with regardless of who the Democratic nominee is. Republican voters need to scout whom they want for their own team, and be proud of that pick, rather than tailor their plan based on who the Left chooses. It's not time to play the whining-baby, always complaining about cheating instead of focusing on the game. It's time to go on the offensive.

If they are going to defeat Clinton – the overwhelming Dem favorite – they will need to select a candidate who is comfortable in his or her own skin, can relate to the cares and concerns of everyday people, oozes charisma, and can articulate a positive agenda for moving the country forward. In short, Republicans need a very strong candidate if they are going to win back the White House in 2016.

First String:

1. Sen. Marco Rubio (R-FL)

☑ **Strengths**: Early favorite of establishment Republicans; has been dubbed the "Republican Savior." On paper Rubio makes sense: A Hispanic (Cuban) from the most important electoral swing-state (Florida) for Republicans in the general election. Represents the face of the next generation of Republicans moving forward. Charismatic speaker who, though he fumbled the 2013 State of the Union response, must summon the voice he had when he delivered a crowd-pleasing speech at the Reagan Presidential Library in 2011. With the full delegate voting status of the Florida primary restored in 2016, his home state will likely offer more weight to his bid for the nomination.

☑ **Weaknesses**: Lacks gubernatorial experience, and as U.S. Senator has potentially tough votes looming on the horizon. Potential vetting issues could haunt him in the general election (not just his personal biography but his time in the Florida House of Representatives – he had several ethics violations, like using the state GOP credit card to purchase groceries, repair his family's car, and buy his wife a plane ticket.)

☑ **Keep An Eye On**: Immigration reform – Now that he has inextricably tied himself to establishment Republican efforts on immigration reform, a subpar bill could put Rubio crosswise with the conservative base, particularly in the early nominating contests.

2. **Gov. Chris Christie (R-NJ)**

☑ **Strengths**: Successful governor from arctic-blue state. Fantastic crossover appeal that is literally worth Christie's weight in gold. Oozes that "anti-Mitt Romney" vibe – he gives off a "just like you and me" impression. Whether slow jamming with Jimmy Fallon, working over David Letterman or poking fun about his vaunted fleece, Christie understands how to use the media to his advantage. At this stage, some polls even have Christie ahead of Clinton in key 2016 battleground states like Colorado.[119]

☑ **Weaknesses**: What makes Christie popular with Democrats and independents is also his Achilles' heel with the Republican base. From his hug and "bromance" with Obama during the 2012 presidential campaign to his whiny plea for funds as a result of Superstorm Sandy to his snafu over the special election to replace deceased Senator Frank Lautenberg to palling it up with Bill Clinton in Chicago – Christie has a lot of fences to mend if he is going to win the GOP nomination. As several pundits have pointed out Christie may be a frontrunner for the nomination, the only question is: for which party? It may not be polite to say, but Christie still has to drop a lot more weight. New Jersey may accept a hefty chief executive but America likes 'em trimmer.[120]

☑ **Keep An Eye On**: Does Christie win re-election in New Jersey by more than 20-points? And how do the 2014 midterms turnout for Republicans? If the answer to the first question is "yes" and the second question is "poorly" – the GOP may be desperate enough to nominate Lucifer if it they think it will give them a fighting chance in 2016. Christie has said he will make his decision on a presidential run in 2015. My sources say much sooner.

3. Gov. Scott Walker (R-WI)

☑ **Strengths**: A Midwestern governor who appeals to blue-collar voters and to the religious right. Positioned to be a strong sleeper candidate in the 2016 presidential primary should he throw his hat into the ring. A darling of fiscal conservatives for effectively repealing union collective bargaining rights in Wisconsin and who raised $30 million to fend off a state-wide recall election. Walker has shown remarkable political durability in a state that Republicans haven't won on the national level since 1984.

☑ **Weaknesses**: A prime target for "war on women" Democratic motif and unions in the general election. Not exactly seen as the most charismatic guy in the world on the stump, often likened to former Minnesota Gov. Tim Pawlenty. No guarantee that he will deliver Wisconsin in the general election. Needs to raise his profile outside of the conservative base.

☑ **Keep an eye on**: If Walker can achieve a sizable margin of victory in his 2014   gubernatorial   re-election bid, strategists and fundraisers will likely flock to his camp.

4. Sen. Rand Paul (R-KY)

☑ **Strengths**: A favorite among libertarian and tea partiers. Largely inherits his father's supporters, which could be extremely beneficial in the early nominating contests. Has successfully boosted name ID by harping on constitutional issues (drones, NSA, etc.). Has demonstrated ability to raise money on a national scale and, thanks to his father's loyal army of followers, is believed to have a strong early organizational advantage over the rest of the potential 2016 field.[121]

☑ **Weaknesses**: Being Dr. Ron Paul's son (a strength can be a weakness – just Google "Ron Paul" and "newsletters" to find a lot of baggage). Rand's esoteric rants at times leave some wondering if he is all there. Being a first-term U.S. Senator, he lacks executive experience. Needs to find a way to broaden his appeal among establishment Republicans.

☑ **Keep an eye on:** Can Rand Paul effectively marry his constitutional libertarian philosophy with practical governing on a national scale?

Second String:

1. Former Gov. Jeb Bush (R-FL)

☑ **Strengths**: Popular governor with a solid conservative record from the most important swing state.

Outspoken on immigration and education reform – two issues Republicans need to make inroads on in the general election. Has near-universal access to fundraising. Married to a Mexican-American. Well versed in conveying complex issues and making them palpable for everyday folks.

☑ **Weaknesses**: If Jeb's last name were not Bush he would probably already be sitting in the White House and certainly at the top of the GOP contender list in 2016. Rusty re-entry into possible 2016 presidential run with a slip on immigration. Not sure he is mentally prepared for the presidential campaign trail. Inter-family dynamics could force him not to run (wife, children, extended family).

☑ **Keep an eye on**: Media will be pushing for a made-in-Hollywood general election race: Bush v. Clinton. How improved are George W. Bush's numbers and image as Obama's second term continues? This will be key.

2. **Rep. Paul Ryan (R-WI)**

☑ **Strengths**: As Mitt Romney's VP nominee in 2012, he has general election campaign experience. Very popular with the conservative base. As Chairman of House Budget Committee, he sits at the nexus of what interests conservatives the most (fiscal responsibility).

☑ **Weaknesses**: Not a strong campaigner. Couldn't carry Wisconsin for Romney. Still green as a stump speaker and comes off as a little wonky. Member of House of Representatives (James A. Garfield in 1880 was last sitting House member to make the leap to the Oval Office).[122]

☑ **Keep an eye on:** Not sure that he is actually all that interested in running. May signal as much early.

3. **Unknown (A 2014 Midterm Success Story)**

☑ **Strengths**: Fresh buzz and an unknown commodity that could pique the interest of rank-and-file voters. Could be riding the wave of the midterms if Republicans are successful.

☑ **Weaknesses**: Will be behind in organization and likely won't have national fundraising spigot or name ID to tap.

☑ **Keep an eye on**: The 2014 midterms. Someone could come out of the woodwork (Think, Obama).

4. **Gov. Bobby Jindal (R-LA)**

☑ **Strengths**: Diversity (Indian American). Southern governor with a strong resume. Chairman of the Republican Governors Association.

☑ **Weaknesses**: Terrible in state polling amid controversial second term. Weak stump speaker. Badly fumbled 2009 State of the Union response.

☑ **Keep an eye on:** Jindal's poll numbers in Louisiana; if they don't drastically improve he won't get much traction in the national conversation. Could find himself on the short list for VP in 2016.

Third String:

1. **Sen. Ted Cruz (R-TX)**

☑ **Strengths**: Conservative voting record: "The golden boy" of the far right who doesn't seem threatened by establishment Republicans or the Democratic machine. Polls well with conservatives and Republicans who know who he is. A fresh face of Hispanic (Cuban) heritage, without the same personal baggage as Rubio. Is making the rounds in person and on TV – working the national political-media complex like an established fiddle player.[123]

☑ **Weaknesses**: Newbie – elected to the U.S. Senate in 2012. Seen by many as a political arsonist with a tendency to create enemies at every turn, particularly in the Senate. Limited appeal beyond tea party.

☑ **Keep an eye on**: How much he tamps down his "fire and brimstone" rhetoric. Also, born in Canada, not entirely clear he is eligible to run for president.

2. **Former Sen. Rick Santorum (R-PA)**

☑ **Strengths**: Technically, the "next in line" – runner-up in 2012 to the eventual GOP presidential nominee Mitt Romney. Generates strong support from social conservatives and blue-collar primary goers. On campaign trail, has figured out how to turn nothing into something and survive off the land.

☑ **Weaknesses**: Incendiary statements. Doesn't always think before he speaks. Faces a much more talented and crowded 2016 field. In other words, he is not taking aim at a stationary target like Mitt Romney. May have perseverance but Santorum is becoming synonymous with losing big (Think, 2006 PA Senate race).

☑ **Keep an eye on**: How much time he spends in Iowa, the state that propelled him into the spotlight in 2012.

3. **Gov. Susana Martinez (R-NM)**

☑ **Strengths**: A border-state chief executive of Hispanic (Mexican) heritage in a left-leaning state with strong crossover appeal. She has a fiscally conservative record and has managed to improve social services in New Mexico. As the first Hispanic female governor in the country, Martinez plugs two of the three holes Republicans have in terms of winning the White House (women, Hispanics). Gave a solid speech at the 2012 GOP convention.

☑ **Weaknesses**: Low national name ID. Does not appear interested in running for president in 2016. Supported Medicaid expansion. Up for re-election as governor in 2014.

☑ **Keep an eye on**: The more people get to know her the more they like her, particularly donors. Martinez might be the best-positioned candidate to complement a Republican ticket as VP in recent memory – aka the perfect VP.

4. **Gov. Rick Perry (R-TX)**

☑ **Strengths**: Longest serving governor in Texas history. Presides over strongest state economy in U.S. Known as a job creator. A true competitor, irked by poor showing in 2012 GOP presidential primary.

☑ **Weaknesses**: Terrible debater – "Oops!" Hard to forget sloppy, mistake-filled run for the White House in 2012.

☑ **Keep An Eye On**: Perry's decision not to seek re-election as Texas governor in 2014 indicates that he is seriously contemplating a second run at the White House.

BONUS SECTION: SIX WAYS TO BEAT HILLARY CLINTON + 2-PT CONVERSION

The sheer amount of evidence that Hillary Clinton is gearing up for a 2016 presidential run should sound alarms. The super PAC anticipating her run, "Ready For Hillary," is moving at full speed. It has attracted prominent Democratic operatives like Harold Ickes and James Carville, and has begun the fundraising groundwork necessary for a long-haul candidacy. Behind the scenes, Democratic strategists are already beginning the transition from President Obama to Hillary as speaking requests flood in for the former First Lady. At a rate in the neighborhood of $200,000 per speech, Clinton is getting the speaking practice she needs. Beyond her physical presence, her online presence has been ramped up. The former Senator and Secretary of State has already taken to

Twitter so that she can weigh in on the conversation, with her account listing her previous experience and an ominous "TBD." A new Clinton memoir is slated to be released in the summer of 2014, paired with a movie, tentatively scheduled for 2016 release, entitled "Rodham" focusing on her early days as a young lawyer in Washington D.C. Stepping away from the Obama administration has not meant that Hillary has abandoned her policy involvement. Her newfound work with the Clinton Global Initiative should help give her an edge when weighing in on the pressing social issues of the day.

While all of these signals should have the GOP gearing up for a big fight, they also mean that the GOP has an advantage if it plays its cards right; or rather, plays its game plan right. The greatest upsets in NFL history have a common theme: the Goliaths that have fallen were all too well-known ahead of time, while the Davids have flown in under the radar. This doesn't mean that the "miracle" team is without talent; points must be scored and steamrolling offenses must be stalled for the upset to occur. But when a team stacked with star players and carrying the publicity of an entire season walks into the stadium, the challengers know exactly what battle they are in for. The 8-7 Minnesota Vikings shocked the 13-2 San Francisco 49ers in the 1988 playoffs by having the right formula to shut down Joe Montana. The Hall of Fame quarterback was benched in that loss. The defending champion Green Bay Packers, led by season MVP Brett Favre, found their usual game plan thwarted by the aging

Denver Broncos in Super Bowl XXXII. And who can forget the performance of the New York Giants' defensive line in collapsing the comfortable pocket that had helped Tom Brady lead the New England Patriots to an 18-0 record. The Giants' Super Bowl XLII win had its fair share of "miracles," but they were only made possible by a Giants defense that had plenty of games to study their opponent's offensive mojo.

It would be a gross understatement to say that Hillary Clinton has the Big Mo. Bloomberg's Al Hunt claims that right now Clinton is the strongest frontrunner ever.[124] And yes, when it comes to 2016, Republicans should be seriously concerned that Democrats could lock off the White House for another eight years. Mrs. Clinton may not technically be on the same plane as an incumbent president seeking re-election, but in the open-seat era she is a pretty strong favorite for 2016 – perhaps by two to three touchdowns. But she is also a favorite who is familiar, exposed, and perhaps overconfident.

Can she be beat? Yes. Will it be easy? No. What do Republicans need, other than a warehouse full of Ouija boards? A strong, charismatic presidential nominee to score the points, and a well-executed game plan to derail a steamrolling Hillary campaign. Below is the blueprint for such a plan.

1. Raise Expectations ... Before She Lowers Them
Make no mistake about it; Hillary Clinton has begun her march toward the White House at an even earlier date

than she did for 2008. Accordingly, one of Team Clinton's biggest worries is that the early behind-the-scenes activity will force her hand before they can devise a strong path to victory. This fear – hidden behind a screen of confidence and endorsements – is what Republicans need to exploit with focus and force. They need to make a surprise move across the aisle to join the retinue of Democrats in showing that Hillary Clinton is without question running for president. If the GOP can add fuel to the fire of "Hillary mania," then everything that she does from this day until the Iowa caucuses can be viewed by the public as cynically geared toward winning the 2016 election.

What Team Clinton wants to do is keep a low profile and manage expectations between now and the 2014 midterms, then slowly kick Hillary mania into overdrive about 20 minutes after the midterms conclude. This is a luxury that the GOP cannot freely give. The deep longing for a Clinton presidency from the Democratic sidelines can be played to Republicans' advantage if they heed the advice of Republican operative Ed Rogers – make Hillary mania "tiresome" long before it is ready to take the political world by storm.[125] Democrats are already assisting. Senator Claire McCaskill, who distanced herself from the Clintons in 2006 when she said about Bill, "I think he's been a great leader, but I don't want my daughter near him," has already endorsed Hillary for 2016. Others have followed suit.[126]

The conservative pundit class should lead the charge in drawing attention to Hillary mania, taking every opportunity to critique Clinton's motives and make clear her planned candidacy. They should exploit Clinton's belief that she is preordained to sit in the Oval Office and that her entire career has been manufactured to meet this objective. Her allies will try to turn Hillary 2.0 into History 2.0; the nation's first African-American president followed by the nation's first female president. She must be denied this avenue. This is not about a desire to see more women in public office; this is about Hillary and her own unfettered ambitions. When she officially makes her announcement, the media should be collectively yawning. When Mrs. Clinton gives her victory speech at the Iowa caucuses in 2016, media scrutiny should be so strong that if her victory speech is not the modern-day equivalent of the Gettysburg address, it will be viewed as a resounding failure.

2. Stay Out of Her Bedroom

There are few things that Republicans and conservatives enjoy more than poking fun at Bill and Hillary Clinton's "professional" marriage and the assorted outside "trysts" that have marred it. But for the love of all that is holy, Republicans must stay out of her bedroom.

Infidelity and sexual scandals just do not hold the same water they used to among the voting public. Take Anthony Weiner's campaign for New York mayor, former South Carolina Governor Mark Sanford's election to the House, or Eliot Spitzer's media deals. While their sexual misdeeds certainly matter to some voters, they do not for most. We have entered an age when politicians of all stripes are caught engaging in behavior that would make a reality TV producer blush. Consequently, voters' tolerance for misdeeds has sparked a rush for redemption. The political risks of making this an issue outweigh any of the potential benefits. Focusing on bedroom issues could alienate the unmarried female voters and young voters whose support drove Barack Obama's election victories.

That doesn't mean that Republicans can leave this to the domain of Rush Limbaugh and conservative talkers either. A significant number of voters cannot make the distinction between a radio personality and a political candidate. We saw this in 2012 when Rush Limbaugh's attacks on Sandra Fluke were used against Mitt Romney's campaign. With the help of Democratic propaganda peddlers, it is far too easy for the eventual GOP standard-bearer to be weighed down by the comments of those who cannot resist a Monica Lewinsky joke 15+ years after the fact. Former Republican Congressman-turned-TV-host Joe Scarborough is right: "We just can't confuse … political entertainment with what draws people to the polls."[127]

Democrats don't like to talk substance. They prefer to play games with an American public that just doesn't follow the "Beltway Beat" with an insider's regularity. Republicans cannot afford to walk headlong into this trap. At risk is a fictitious yet powerful "War on Women II" meme that could bog down both the candidate and his or her base. Republicans and right-leaning media need to resist this urge, or they will find themselves making bedroom jokes about Bill home alone in the White House for another four years.

3. Let Bill Self-Destruct

Speaking of Bill, he is not the albatross for Hillary Clinton that many Republicans hope he will be. While many moderates and independent voters may loathe a third Obama term, they would happily welcome a third Clinton term because "it's the economy, stupid." Digging into his presidential record and personal baggage will prove to be a largely futile exercise when voters can point to American economic success during his presidency.

But that doesn't mean Bill Clinton cannot be a godsend for the Republican Party as they face his wife. As Bloomberg's Margaret Carlson notes, Bill Clinton loves the spotlight. Narcissus has met his match in Bill. No politician has more of a public desire to be admired or a greater passion to be proven right. When the spotlight shines on him for long periods of time, he has a tendency to get "carried away.[128] The key is not digging up old dirt, but looking for the fresh material and angles that will undoubtedly arise.

So how do Republicans shine a spotlight on Bill so that his shadow looms large over her campaign at all the wrong times? Republicans need him to second-guess Hillary's campaign tactics and policy positions at every turn. This will remind people ever so subtly that she is just not him – and neither are her policies. Hillary stood by her man; now it is time to make Bill choose. Team Obama understood this very well in 2008, particularly as it related to the South Carolina primary. When the Hillary campaign wanted to declare South Carolina a lost cause and focus their efforts on potential gains elsewhere, Bill didn't like the plan – and said so. "He thought it was crazy not to spend every day in South Carolina," a top aide said. "He thought he could make it close." [129] But after a series of questionable comments by Bill and far too much face time, Hillary lost big in the state and soon found herself watching Obama pummel Senator John McCain from the sidelines. Bill has rained on his wife's parade before. There's plenty of reason to believe that, under the spotlight, he would do so again.

4. Foggy Bottom Breakdown: A Lack of Competence, Character & Leadership

If you listen closely to the Obama-centric mainstream media, one would think that the President's choice of Hillary Clinton as Secretary of State was a match made in policy heaven, while also meeting Obama's need to neutralize his chief earthly rival. But the truth is that Hillary needed Obama more than he needed her. Hillary needed a way to step out of Bill's shadow, and this job opening gave her that chance. Yes, Hillary supporters fawn over her record at Foggy Bottom as evidence that she is ready to lead this nation. They cite that she has visited a record number of countries and traveled a record number of miles as America's top diplomat. But a closer look reveals a very different picture. A record number of carries does not mean that a running back gained positive yards, let alone scored the winning touchdown.

Mrs. Clinton was certainly "industrious" in her time at Foggy Bottom, but she hardly had a distinguished record as

Secretary of State. As Fox News' Brit Hume points out, there is no specific "Clinton Doctrine" on foreign policy.[130] She did not pioneer a new grand strategy. In fact, she went along with the Administration's vision of "leading from behind." As for specific accomplishments: Is the Middle East any closer to peace? Has there been any real headway on shutting down the Iranian and North Korean nuclear programs? Has the re-set with Russia worked? Are there major new treaties she can point to? The answer to all of these questions is a resounding no.

If you peel back the onion even more you might admit that her tenure as Secretary of State was eventful – in terms of scandals, that is. Benghazi revealed Clinton's inability to adequately protect her own diplomats in Libya (incompetence) and exposed the multiple lies told about the attack to protect her political image (character). Reports that the State Department spent hundreds of thousands of dollars to buy "likes" on Facebook, while more trivial, are easy to understand and exemplify waste in government. Allegations of rampant sexual misconduct within the State Department, revealed in an internal Office of Inspector General memo and reported by major news outlets, were also harmful to her record as a leader. When combined with her insistence on silence, they could be just as harmful to her record on women's rights.

Despite the rosy picture Clinton supporters and the media try to paint regarding her time as Secretary of State, Hillary has a lot to answer for. If the media won't ask the questions, Republicans must pick up the ball.

5. A Washington Insider With a Questionable Record

Moving away from Foggy Bottom, one of the key selling points for a Hillary Clinton presidency is that her candidacy represents something "distinct and historic."[131] Under no circumstances should Republicans and the eventual GOP presidential nominee allow her to successfully build that case. No successful game plan involves allowing the team to play to their strengths. As UVA politics professor Larry Sabato notes, "[T]here is going to be a strong desire on the Left to elect the nation's first woman president."[132] Republicans need to turn that around and play to the strong desire in the country to elect the first competent president in recent history.

While the Democrats may play up the "history" of a Hillary candidacy, there is nothing historic or new about her Washington ties. She has been hanging around the Beltway since the 1970s, making herself at home in the comfortable Washington circles that are geared to sucking up and self-promotion, not to successfully improving the nation.

Voters on the Left and Right share one quality: They despise Washington, seeing it as arrogant, incompetent and insular. Hillary personifies these qualities. Her statement during the Senate hearings on the Benghazi attacks – "What difference, at this point, does it make?" – was anything but compassionate and empathetic. In fact, it was the opposite: callous and indifferent.[133]

So Clinton's insider experience can and must be turned into a major liability. In this era of great distrust of government, the Clinton political machine's record in Washington cannot go untouched.

Ironically, the candidate whose game plan was most effective in exploiting Hillary's insider record was Barack Obama. He argued in 2008 that "[i]f Hillary Clinton is the nominee, then we have a repetition of 2000 and 2004."[134] Harping on how she voted along the lines of the Bush administration proved incredibly effective, even if the similarities were exaggerated. His attack also sent a signal to voters that if this Beltway veteran were the nominee, the partisan bickering of the past two decades would continue unabated.

Conversely, Mitt Romney, a true Washington outsider, failed to exploit this advantage. He rarely tied Barack Obama to the dysfunctional city he worked in for eight years and led for four. Consequently, Washington's unpopularity rarely rubbed off on the President.

The goal here is simple: Turn Hillary Clinton's lengthy experience into a liability. No matter how you slice it, most Democrats are going to vote for her because she is a "brand name." Republicans need to tamp down enthusiasm for Hillary and shine a light on her Washington baggage in much the same way that Obama did with Romney's business record. This has the potential to create doubt among independents and moderates. Beating Clinton in a general election will take near-flawless execution at the voting margins. Focusing elsewhere – straying from the game plan – means letting Hillary play to her own fictitious strengths.

6. Holding Hillary to Her Own Rules

Secretary Clinton may not have been involved in the IRS's harassment of conservative organizations, the Justice Department's seizure of journalists' telephone records, or the Fast and Furious cover-up. But this doesn't mean those scandals cannot be used against her. All violate President Obama's own pledge to promote trust and transparency within the federal government.

Here, the Republicans have the opportunity to take a page out of Hillary mentor Saul Alinsky's book. In *Rules for Radicals*, Alinsky advocates "making the enemy live up to its own book of rules."[135] Every unmet Obama campaign promise represents a rule that's been broken. And it is fair political game to make Hillary defend or deny them.

Every presidential candidate seeks to create distance from the most unpopular or notorious aspects of their predecessor's record. As the National Journal's Josh Kraushaar notes, "Public dissatisfaction with George W. Bush made Democratic Party voters look for someone disconnected from the decision to go to war with Iraq."[136] Hillary just didn't cut it.

A decade earlier, then-Vice President Al Gore tried to create space between him and his former boss's sex scandal, going so far as to select Clinton critic Senator Joe Lieberman as his running mate. Despite voters' approval of Clinton's policies, he didn't get far enough away.

The GOP now has the chance to punish Hillary for her decision to jump onboard the Obama train. Just a few months ago, it seemed obvious that the 2016 Democratic nominee would be running on Obama's legacy. Now the outlook is more dubious. Republicans cannot let Hillary get the best of both worlds: Being a relatively meaningful part of the Obama administration but staying distant enough to avoid its major downfalls.

Think about how Obama turned Bush's record into McCain's. The "more of the same" argument was kryptonite to the helpless Senator. Tie Obama's scandals to Hillary and argue that America cannot afford four more years of the same arrogant executive power abuses and broken promises.

Two-Point Conversion: "Pray For Primary Opponents"

It is Hillary Clinton's intention to clear the Democratic presidential primary field before the race even begins. As the overwhelming media favorite, she wants to avoid being knocked around in the way the not-ready-for-primetime cast of Republican underdogs pounced on Romney in 2012. At the end of the day, the damage that the 2012 Republican field did to Romney was Obama's best weapon against him in a relatively close election.

For this reason, Republicans need to hope that a credible cast of characters (Biden, Booker, Dean, Cuomo, Gillibrand, Klobuchar, M. Obama, O'Malley, Warren) decides to throw caution to the wind and jumps in. The reason: Republicans need real-time data on what makes the Democratic base cringe about Hillary. It's opposition research done by the opposition. After all, the only thing better than following your own game plan is finding yourself in possession of the other team's playbook.

ABOUT THE AUTHOR

Ford O'Connell is a political analyst and a Republican strategist. A seasoned campaign veteran at the local, state and national levels, Mr. O'Connell worked on the 2008 McCain-Palin presidential campaign.

In 2010, *Campaigns & Elections* magazine named Mr. O'Connell a "Rising Star." A frequent on-air guest on Fox News, CNN and other broadcast media, his political commentary has appeared in a variety of publications including *USA Today*, the Associated Press, Reuters, *The Washington Post*, *Washington Times*, *New York Daily News*, *U.S. News & World Report*, *The Hill*, *POLITICO*, *Investor's Business Daily*, E! Online, *People* magazine and ESPN.com.

Mr. O'Connell earned a Juris Doctor from the University of Virginia School of Law and holds graduate degrees from Duke University, Northwestern University and the

University of Mississippi. He received his undergraduate degree from Swarthmore College, where he was a member of the football, basketball and lacrosse teams. Mr. O'Connell currently resides in the Washington, D.C. area.

REFERENCES AND CITATIONS

Introduction

[1] Frum, David. "It's the Math." *The Daily Beast.* Newsweek, 9 Nov. 2012.

[2] Sabato, Larry. "12 From '12: Some Takeaways From a Wild Election." *Sabato's Crystal Ball.* UVA Center for Politics, 15 Nov. 2012.

[3] Schwartz, Ian. "George Will To Romney: 'Quit Despising The American People.'" *RealClearPolitics.com.* RealClearPolitics, 18 Nov. 2012.

[4] Newport, Frank. "Alabama, North Dakota, Wyoming Most Conservative States." *Gallup.org.* Gallup Politics, 1 Feb. 2013.

Rule #1: Ronald Reagan is Dead. Accept It.

[5] "Reagan Lies in State at Capitol." *BBCNews.com.* BBC News, 11 June 2004.

[6] Davis, Susan. "McCain, Romney Unveil New Attack Ads." *Washington Wire.* The Wall Street Journal, 4 Feb. 2008.

[7] Cooper, Michael, and Michael Luo. "Romney and McCain Tangle at Debate, but Also Try to Mold a Two-Man Race." *NYTimes.com*. The New York Times, 31 Jan. 2008.

[8] Rafferty, Andrew. "In New Hampshire, McCain Talks up Romney's Foreign Policy Cred." *NBCNews.com*. NBC News, 17 Sept. 2012.

Rule #2: Stop Giving a Shit About Obama's Birthplace (and Obama altogether)

[9] Pedulla, Tom. "NFL's Franchise of the Decade? 3 Super Wins Give It to Patriots." *USAToday.com*. USA Today, 17 Feb. 2010.

[10] "Presidential Race Dead Even; Romney Maintains Turnout Edge." *PewResearch.org*. Pew Research Center, 29 Oct. 2012.

[11] Thomas, Cal. "Hating Obama Is Not a Winning Policy." *MDJOnline.com*. Marietta Daily Journal, 5 Mar. 2013.

[12] Krauthammer, Charles. "Bush Derangement Syndrome." *Townhall.com*. Townhall, 5 Dec. 2003. Web. 2 July 2013.

[13] Jones, Jeffrey M. "Obama Averages 49% Approval in First Term." *Gallup.org*. Gallup Politics, 21 Jan. 2013.

[14] "American President: Franklin Delano Roosevelt: Campaigns and Elections." *MillerCenter.org*. Miller Center, University of Virginia.

[15] Stephey, M.J. "Top 10 Memorable Debate Moments: Reagan's Age-Old Wisdom." *Time.com*. Time Magazine, n.d.

[16] Blake, Aaron. "Palin delights CPAC crowd with string of Obama one-liners." *WashingtonPost.com*. The Washington Post, 16 Mar. 2013.

[17] Wilson, Scott, and Philip Rucker. "Stymied by a GOP House, Obama Looks Ahead to 2014 to Cement His Legacy." *WashingtonPost.com*. The Washington Post, 2 Mar. 2013.

[18] Todd, Chuck, Mark Murray, Domenic Montanaro, and Brooke Bower. "First Thoughts: Different Attitude Greeting Obama's Upcoming Inaugural." *NBCNews.com*. NBC News, 18 Jan. 2013.

Rule #3: Roe v. Wade is Here to Stay

[19] Jones, Jeffrey M. "Gender Gap in 2012 Vote Is Largest in Gallup's History." *Gallup.org*. Gallup Politics, 9 Nov. 2012.

[20] Dailey, Kate. "US Election: Women Are the New Majority." *BBCNews.com*. BBC, 11 July 2012.

[21] "A Look at the Changing Makeup of US Electorate." *Newsmax.com*. Newsmax, 10 Nov. 2012.

[22] "Unmarried America: How They Get News & Information." *VoterParticipation.org*. Voter Participation Center, 22 Aug. 2012.

[23] "Roe v. Wade at 40: Most Oppose Overturning Abortion Decision - Pew Forum on Religion & Public Life." *PewForum.org*. Pew Research Center, 16 Jan. 2013.

[24] Cooper, Michael. "G.O.P. Approves Strict Anti-abortion Language in Party Platform." *NYTimes.com*. The New York Times, 21 Aug. 2012.

25 Saad, Lydia. "Majority of Americans Still Support Roe v. Wade Decision." *Gallup.org*. Gallup Politics, 22 Jan. 2013.

26 Blake, Aaron. "Todd Akin, GOP Senate Candidate: 'Legitimate Rape' Rarely Causes Pregnancy." *The Fix*. The Washington Post, 19 Aug. 2012.

27 Madison, Lucy. "Richard Mourdock: Even Pregnancy from Rape Something "God Intended"." *CBSNews.com*. CBS News, 23 Oct. 2012.

Rule #4: Hug the Gays (No, Really)

28 "2004 Election Exit Polls." *CNN.com*. Cable News Network, n.d.

29 Terkel, Amanda. "Gay Voters' Support For Republicans Nearly Doubled From 2008." *TheHuffingtonPost.com*. The Huffington Post, 5 Nov. 2010.

30 Gates, Gary J. "How Many People Are Lesbian, Gay, Bisexual and Transgender?" *WilliamsInstitute.law.ucla.edu*. The Williams Institute, Apr. 2011.

31 "Post-ABC Poll: Jason Collins, Gay Marriage and Boy Scouts." *WashingtonPost.com*. The Washington Post, 9 May 2013.

32 "In Gay Marriage Debate, Both Supporters and Opponents See Legal Recognition as 'Inevitable.'" *People-Press.org*. Pew Research Center, 6 June 2013.

33 Cillizza, Chris. "Why the Political Fight on Gay Marriage Is over — in 3 Charts." *WashingtonPost.com*. The Washington Post, 25 Mar. 2013.

[34] Murray, Mark. "NBC/WSJ Poll: 53 Percent Support Gay Marriage." *NBCNews.com*. NBC News, 11 Apr. 2013.

[35] Burnett, Sara. "Illinois Republican Party chairman Pat Brady survives latest ouster attempt after gay-marriage flap." *Chicago Sun-Times.com*. Chicago Sun-Times, 13 Apr. 2013.

[36] NBC News/Wall Street Journal survey, Study #13127. *NBCNews.com*. NBC News, The Wall Street Journal, 5-8 Apr. 2013.

[37] Cohen, Micah. "Gay Vote Proved a Boon for Obama." *FiveThirtyEight*. The New York Times, 15 Nov. 2012.

[38] Silver, Nate. "How Opinion on Same-Sex Marriage Is Changing, and What It Means." *FiveThirtyEight*. The New York Times, 26 Mar. 2013.

[39] Goldberg, Jonah. "Abortion and Gay Marriage: Separate Issues." *National Review Online*. National Review, 22 Mar. 2013.

[40] "Gay Vote Proved a Boon for Obama."

[41] Gates, Gary, and Frank Newport." LGBT Americans Skew Democratic, Largely Support Obama." *Gallup.org*. Gallup Politics, 18 Oct. 2012.

[42] Casselman, Ben. "Number of the Week: Youth Unemployment at 22.9%?" *WSJ.com*. The Wall Street Journal, 6 Apr. 2013.

[43] Rovzar, Chris. "Michele Bachmann's Problem With Gay People Could Soon Become a Problem for Her." *NYMag.com*. New York Magazine, 13 July 2011.

Rule #5: Kill Immigration Reform, Kill the GOP

[44] "Top 10 Joe Biden Gaffes." *Time.com*. Time Magazine, 17 June 2006.

[45] Safire, William. "Always Shuck the Tamale." Palm Beach Post, 4 May 1976.

[46] "Facts for Features: Hispanic Heritage Month 2012." U.S. Census Bureau, 6 Aug. 2010.

[47] "U.S. Census Bureau Projections Show a Slower Growing, Older, More Diverse Nation a Half Century from Now." U.S. Census Bureau, 12 Dec. 2012.

[48] "Welcome to the New Off-White America." *Fox News Latino*. Fox News, 18 Mar. 2013.

[49] Lopez, Mark H., and Paul Taylor. "Latino Voters in the 2012 Election." *PewHispanic.org*. Pew Research Center, 7 Nov. 2012.

[50] "Latino Influence on 2012 Election: President." *LatinoVoteMap.org*. Latino Decisions, 2012.

[51] Cook, Charlie. "The GOP Keeps Getting Whiter." *NationalJournal.com*. National Journal, 15 Mar. 2013.

[52] "The GOP Keeps Getting Whiter."

[53] Bareto, Matt. "What the GOP Has to Gain – and Lose – among Latinos When It Comes to Immigration Reform." *LatinoDecisions.com*. Latino Decisions. 21 Mar. 2013.

[54] Williams, Juan. "Latinos Make American History, GOP Pays the Bill." *Fox News Latino*. Fox News, 7 Nov. 2012.

[55] "Hispanics in America." *ResurgentRepublic.com*. Resurgent Republic, 2012.

[56] "Census Bureau Reports Hispanic-Owned Businesses Increase at More Than Double the National Rate." U.S. Census Bureau, 21 Sept. 2010.

[57] Reinhard, Beth. "Haley Barbour: Immigration Bill Isn't Going to Change Many Hispanic Voters' Minds." *NationalJournal.com.* National Journal, 21 Mar. 2013.

[58] Warren, Michael. "Getting to Sí." *WeeklyStandard.com.* The Weekly Standard, 12 July 2013.

[59] Llorente, Elizabeth. "Immigration Hardliner Popular With Latinos Tapped By GOP As Model Candidate." *Fox News Latino.* Fox News, 21 Mar. 2013.

[60] Olsen, Henry. "American Enterprise Institute." *NYPost.com.* New York Post, 9 Nov. 2012.

[61] "Welcome to the New Off-White America."

Rule #6: Leave the Sideshows to Donald Trump

[62] "Election 2012: Results." *CNN.com.* Cable News Network, 10 Dec. 2012.

[63] Jeansonne, John. "The Unique Style of John Gagliardi." *Newsday.com.* Newsday, 26 Nov. 2012.

[64] Stein, Sam. "Jon Huntsman: GOP Primary Barriers To Entry Were 'Pretty Damn Low'" *TheHuffingtonPost.com.* The Huffington Post, 28 Nov. 2012.

[65] Glueck, Katie. "Reince Priebus: RNC Can Control Debates." *POLITICO.com.* POLITICO, 12 Dec. 2012.

[66] "Bachmann: Repeal Obamacare "Before It Literally Kills Women, Kills Children, Kills Senior Citizens."" *RealClearPolitics.com*. RealClearPolitics, 21 Mar. 2013.

[67] Weinger, Mackenzie. "Ron Paul Calls Newt Gingrich a 'chickenhawk'." *POLITICO.com*. POLITICO, 4 Jan. 2012.

[68] Huisenga, Sarah. "Herman Cain Acknowledges His Electric Border Fence Idea Isn't a Joke after All." *CBSNews.com*. CBS News, 17 Oct. 2011.

[69] Huisenga, Sarah. "Cain Says He's Ready for Questions About 'Ubeki-beki-beki-beki-stan-stan.'" *NationalJournal.com*. National Journal, 10 Oct. 2011.

[70] "6 Newt Gingrich Soundbites That Will Hurt Mitt Romney in November." *TheWeek.com*. The Week, 10 Apr. 2012.

[71] "Rick Perry's Debate 'Oops' and More of His Biggest Blunders." *The Daily Beast*. Newsweek, 11 Nov. 2011.

[72] O'Brien, Michael. "Santorum Sharpens Attacks on Romney to Include Bain Record." *NBCNews.com*. NBC News, 13 Mar. 2012.

[73] Sands, Geneva. "Santorum Steps up Rhetoric: Romney 'doesn't Have a Core'." *TheHill.com*. The Hill, 19 Mar. 2012.

[74] "February 2012 Purple Poll." *PurpleStrategies.com*. Purple Strategies, Feb. 2012.

[75] Montanaro, Domenico, and Carrie Dann. "As Primary War Wages, Romney's Support with Independents Dips." *NBCNews.com*. NBC News, 30 Jan. 2012.

[76] Montopoli, Brian. "Poll: Obama Holds Edge over GOP Hopefuls." *CBSNews.com*. CBS News, 14 Feb. 2012.

Rule #7: It's All About the Q

[77] Smith, Stephen. "NFL's Top 100 Players of All-Time: Debate." *CBSNews.com*. CBS News, 5 Nov. 2010.

[78] Michael, Ryan. "Joe Namath Is the Most Overrated Player in NFL History." *BleacherReport.com*. Bleacher Report, 10 Nov. 2008.

[79] Kelly, Heather. "Oscar Night's Highs and Lows on Twitter." *CNN.com*. Cable News Network, 25 Feb. 2013.

[80] Rothman, Noah. "Obama Overtakes Reagan As Most Televised President In History." *Mediaite.com*. Mediaite, 23 Apr. 2012.

[81] Bierly, Mandi. "Pauley Perrette as Appealing as Tom Hanks and Morgan Freeman? Kinda Awesome." *EW.com*. Entertainment Weekly, 22 Mar. 2010.

[82] Prior, Markus. "Media and Political Polarization." *Annual Review of Political Science* (2013): 101-27.

[83] "Obama's soft-media strategy." *POLITICO.com*. POLITICO, 17 Aug. 2012.

[84] "TV Ratings." *TVbytheNumbers.com*. TVbytheNumbers. com.

[85] O'Connell, Ford. "What Chris Christie Gets About Life and Politics." *USNews.com*. U.S.News & World Report, 9 May 2013.

[86] Sargent, Greg. "How out of touch is today's GOP?" *The Plum Line*. The Washington Post, 16 Apr. 2013.

[87] Newport, Frank. "Hillary Clinton, Barack Obama Most Admired in 2012." *Gallup.org*. Gallup Politics, 31 Dec. 2012.

Rule #8: Never Underestimate Voter Ignorance... and Indifference

[88] Schneider, Matt. "Sen. Schumer: GOP Threat To Shut Down Government Is "Playing With Fire."" *Mediaite.com.* Mediaite, 30 Jan. 2011.

[89] Hume, Brit. "Zogby Poll: Most Americans Can Name Three Stooges, But Not Three Branches of Government." *FoxNews.com.* Fox News, 15 Aug. 2006.

[90] "Filibuster Proof." *PewResearch.org.* Pew Research Center, 2 Feb. 2010.

[91] "What Voters Know about Campaign 2012." People-Press. org. Pew Research Center, 10 Aug. 2012.

[92] "National Geographic-Roper Public Affairs 2006 Geographic Literacy Study." National Geographic Educational Foundation, May 2006.

[93] Grady, Sandy. "Darth Vader Turns into Mary Poppins." The Buffalo News, 9 Oct. 1996.

[94] Associated Press. "Texas Candidate's Comment About Rape Causes a Furor." The New York Times, 26 Mar. 1990.

Rule #9: The Preseason Doesn't Win You the Super Bowl

[95] O'Connell, Ford. "The GOP Needs a New Vocabulary to Win Debt Showdown." *TheHill.com.* The Hill, 15 Jan. 2013.

[96] Sabato, Larry, and Kyle Kondik. "The Early Line on the 2014 Midterms." *WSJ.com*. The Wall Street Journal, 18 Mar. 2013.

[97] "The Early Line on the 2014 Midterms."

[98] Gardner, Page, and Celinda Lake. "Despite 'autopsy,' GOP could have revival in 2014." *POLITICO.com*. POLITICO, 7 Apr. 2013.

[99] "Despite 'autopsy,' GOP Could Have Revival in 2014."

[100] "Despite 'autopsy,' GOP Could Have Revival in 2014."

[101] "2012 Fox News Exit Polls." *FoxNews.com*. Fox News, 6 November 2012.

[102] "2014 Senate Race Ratings." The Cook Political Report, 1 July 2013.

[103] Cook, Charlie. "Long Odds for House Democrats." *NationalJournal.com*. National Journal, 15 July 2013.

[104] Silver, Nate. "Senate Control in 2014 Increasingly Looks Like a Tossup." *FiveThirtyEight*. The New York Times, 15 July 2013.

[105] "Senate Ratings." *RothenbergPoliticalReport.com*. The Rothenberg Political Report, 28 June 2013.

[106] Taylor, Jessica. "Few House Seats up for Grabs In 2014." *MSNBC.com*. MSNBC, 1 May 2013.

[107] "Introducing the 2014 Cook Political Report Partisan Voter Index." *CookPolitical.com*. The Cook Political Report, 4 Apr. 2013.

[108] Schaller, Thomas F. "Democrats Dread 2014 Drop-Off." *Sabato's Crystal Ball*. UVA Center for Politics, 10 Jan. 2013.

[109] Abramowitz, Alan, and Norman Orstein. "Five Myths about Midterm Elections." *WashingtonPost.com*. The Washington Post, 15 Aug. 2010.

[110] Miller, Dan. Detroit Lions Radio, 28 Dec. 2008.

Rule #10:"The 47 Percent" – Not Just a Gaffe, a Prediction

[111] Everson, Darren. "The Game That Changed Alabama." *WSJ.com*. The Wall Street Journal, 4 Dec. 2009.

[112] "Full Transcript of the Mitt Romney Secret Video." *MotherJones.com*. Mother Jones, 19 Sept. 2012.

[113] Murphy, Mike, and Trent Wisecup. "Guest Commentary: Michigan Can Be Testing Ground for a Refocused GOP." *Freep.com*. Detroit Free Press, 7 Apr. 2013.

[114] Silver, Nate. "As Nation and Parties Change, Republicans Are at an Electoral College Disadvantage." *FiveThirtyEight*. The New York Times, 8 Nov. 2012.

[115] Montanaro, Domenico. "Obama Performance with White Voters on Par with Other Democrats." *NBCNews.com*. NBC News, 19 Nov. 2012.

[116] Taylor, Paul. "Politics and Race: Looking Ahead to 2060." *PewResearch.org*. Pew Research Center, 10 May 2013.

[117] "Global Carbon-dioxide Emissions Increase by 1.0 Gt in 2011 to Record High." *IEA.org*. International Energy Agency, 24 May 2012.

[118] Sims, Alex. "How Bear Bryant Became the Branch Rickey of Alabama Football." *BleacherReport.com*. Bleacher Report, 24 Apr. 2013.

2016 Republican Presidential Scouting Report

[119] "Christie, Rubio, Clinton Close In 2016 Colorado Race, Quinnipiac University Poll Finds; Udall Gets Lukewarm Reelection Support For 2014." *Quinnipiac.edu*. Quinnipiac University Polling Institute, 14 June 2013.

[120] "What Chris Christie Gets About Life and Politics."

[121] Hohmann, James. "5 Reasons Why You Should Take Rand Paul Seriously." *POLITICO.com*. POLITICO, 20 Mar. 2013. Web. 19 July 2013.

[122] "From Congress to the White House." *FactCheck.org*. FactCheck.org, 5 Feb. 2008.

[123] Burns, Alexander. "What Ted Cruz Knows." *POLITICO.com*. POLITICO, 2 May 2013.

Bonus Section: Six Ways to Beat Hillary Clinton + 2-Pt Conversion

[124] Hunt, Albert. "Clinton Is Strongest-Ever Frontrunner. If She Runs." *Bloomberg.com*. Bloomberg, 24 Mar. 2013.

[125] Rogers, Ed. "The Insiders: Where Is Hillary Clinton Weak in 2016? It's Not Bill." *WashingtonPost.com*. The Washington Post, 8 Apr. 2013.

[126] Cillizza, Chris. "What Claire McCaskill Wants." *The Fix*. The Washington Post, 18 June 2013.

[127] Poor, Jeff. "Scarborough sounds off on Limbaugh, Drudge, Hannity and Levin." *DailyCaller.com*. The Daily Caller, 19 June 2013.

[128] Carlson, Margaret. "Hillary Has to Dump Bill Now." *Bloomberg.com*. Bloomberg, 18 June 2013.

[129] Simon, Roger. "Part Five: 100 Percent Delusional." *POLITICO.com*. POLITICO, 25 Aug. 2008.

[130] Hume, Brit. "Case For Hillary Clinton 'Being A Great Secretary Of State Is Exceedingly Weak.'" *RealClearPolitics. com*. RealClearPolitics, 27 Jan. 2013.

[131] Zelizer, Julian. "Hillary Clinton and the Experience Trap." *CNN.com*. Cable News Network, 8 Apr. 2013.

[132] Sabato, Larry J., Kyle Kondik, and Geoffrey Skelley. "16 For '16, Part 1: Democrats Again Hunger for History." *Sabato's Crystal Ball*. UVA Center for Politics, 11 Apr. 2013.

[133] Becker, Kyle. "Hillary Clinton's Benghazi Meltdown: What Difference Does It Make?" *IJReview.com*. Independent Journal Review, 23 Jan. 2013.

[134] Kapp, Bonney. "Barack Obama Steps Up Attacks on Hillary Clinton." *FoxNews.com*. Fox News, 28 Oct. 2007.

[135] Alinsky, Saul David. *Rules for Radicals; a Practical Primer for Realistic Radicals*. New York: Random House, 1971.

[136] Kraushaar, Josh. "Hillary Clinton Has the Most to Lose From Obama's Scandals." *NationalJournal.com*. National Journal, 15 May 2013.

5288945R00081

Made in the USA
San Bernardino, CA
02 November 2013